Caught in the Middle

Protecting the Children of High-Conflict Divorce

Carla B. Garrity
Mitchell A. Baris

LEXINGTON BOOKS
An Imprint of Macmillan, Inc.
NEW YORK

Maxwell Macmillan Canada
TORONTO

Maxwell Macmillan International
NEW YORK   OXFORD   SINGAPORE   SYDNEY

Library of Congress Cataloging-in-Publication Data

Garrity, Carla B.
Caught in the middle : protecting the children of high-conflict
divorce / Carla Garrity, Mitchell Baris.
p.   cm.
Includes bibliographical references (p.   ).
ISBN 0-02-911330-X
1. Divorced parents—United States—Psychology.   2. Divorced
parents—United States—Counseling of.   3. Parenting, Part-time—
United States.   4. Children of divorced parents—United States.
5. Custody of children—United States.   I. Baris, Mitchell A.
II. Title.
HQ834.G38   1994
306.89—dc20   93-48210
                                                                          CIP

Lexington Books
An Imprint of Macmillan, Inc.
866 Third Avenue, New York, N.Y. 10022

Maxwell Macmillan Canada, Inc.
1200 Eglinton Avenue East
Suite 200
Don Mills, Ontario M3C 3N1

Macmillan, Inc. is part of the Maxwell Communication
Group of Companies.

Printed in the United States of America

printing number
3   4   5   6   7   8   9   10

Contents

Acknowledgments *v*

1 Introduction *1*
2 Why Work It Out? *11*
3 Understanding Conflict Developmentally *29*
4 How to Assess Conflict *41*
5 Normal Visitation versus Conflict Visitation *51*
6 Identifying and Understanding Parental
  Alienation *65*
7 A Comprehensive Intervention Model
  for Parental Alienation *83*
8 Creating a Parenting Plan for High-
  Conflict Divorce *101*
9 Implementing the Parenting Plan *127*

Appendix A: Parenting Plan *155*
Appendix B: Parenting Checklist *162*
Appendix C: Parenting Coordinator Agreement *168*
Appendix D: Child Therapist Agreement *171*

References *173*
Bibliography *178*
Index *181*

Acknowledgments

To the Boulder and Denver legal and mental health communities, especially the Interdisciplinary Committees on Child Custody, who gave us a professional forum for presenting the earlier and later formulations of these ideas and who helped these ideas to grow, we offer our sincere gratitude.

Thank you to Robert LaCrosse, Robert Hovenden, Stephen White, Cynthia Monahon, and Sandra Rush for the time, knowledge, and special expertise each of them made available to us.

Our families, most of all, inspired, supported, and endured the process with us. To Carla's children Mark, Megan, and Amy, thank you for always sharing a love of books and for respecting my wish to create them. To Mitch's wife, Alexandra, thank you for sharing in my thoughts and offering yours in return. Your support and encouragement are deeply valued.

1

Introduction

Dear Steve,

Why in the devil did you tell the children they could travel alone to your brother's when you don't even know for sure you'll have money for the tickets? Are you out of your mind? I've told you over and over I won't allow Alyssa to travel alone for at least three, maybe four more years. She is too little to be away from both of us for more than one night. As you know, she still has asthma and is very easily upset. Most of all, she doesn't need to spend any time alone with your brother and his rowdy family!

She told me she doesn't even want to go. She's still too scared to spend more than a couple of hours at a friend's house. Matthew is eager to go, of course, and will be very upset if you disappoint him. When will you learn that the children have feelings and start taking them into consideration? That so-called holiday party for needy children you took them to is a great example of your fathering. The children told me how you made them give away the nice gifts my mother had just given them. Terrific!

By the way, the papers you finally sent me from school were so late you mde me miss Alyssa's play that she worked so hard on! I suppose that was an accident too, you are an idiot and a liar, too. And which child did you give permission to go to that

1

science camp? When did you get the feedback from the music teacher—last month? Matthew didn't even bring me his report card until I saw the notice about them. He was afraid to show it to me because you always yell at him about his grades. God, Steve, you and your bimbo don't know a damned thing about raising kids! The children should be applauded for putting up with you. But don't worry, they will learn in time.

As for the school conference schedule, contrary to your ignorant statement, there is no way to meet with the teacher after the Thanksgiving weekend. So I'll take a conference time the first week of November and let you know when it will be. You will let me know if you will be there.

And, For God's sake, don't give me any grief about my taking the kids to Mother's this year like you always do. Your problem is you still think you can control what I do, but you can't. That's over for good; I'm not letting you jerk me around any longer. Just go screw your bimbo if you need to get rid of your stress.

And may I remind you, Steve, that according to our divorce decree I have all the decision-making power for the children's schedule. As for the children missing school if I leave for the winter break early, it will not affect their grades and you know it. If you would stop trying to control everything I do and demanding your own way, maybe we could get along better. At least you could do it for the children's sake!

By the way, I will not pay for any of the travel to your brother's. I can't afford it and I doubt that you can either. You are sure free with money for someone who tells me that he has no income. Don't worry, I've been collecting your old letters and financial statements, and you'll be seeing them all again at the next court hearing.

Love and kisses,
Lori

Dear Lori,

I checked with the school myself. Listed below are eight options to confer with Matthew's teacher after the Thanksgiving weekend. So, as usual, you were lying when you said we had to meet before Thanksgiving. Here they are:

Monday Nov 29 1:20–1:40 P.M.
Monday Nov 29 5:00–5:20 P.M.
Tuesday Nov 30 3:20–3:40 P.M.
Tuesday Nov 30 3:40–4:00 P.M.
Tuesday Nov 30 5:40–6:00 P.M.
Wed Dec 1 3:40–4:00 P.M.
Wed Dec 1 4:00–4:20 P.M.
Wed Dec 1 5:20–5:40 P.M.

Please select from these times and let me know promptly.

Regarding your early departure for winter break I am completely against it. Their report cards should tell you what a disservice you would be doing them. It sends out the wrong message. With that sort of an academic grounding, they will achieve academically exactly as you did—as abysmal failures.

By the way, I don't know where you get the idea I have ever objected to the kids going to your mother's. The fact is that over the past two years I have accommodated to all your scheduling demands so that the children could go when it was convenient for you. Incidentally, Alyssa told me she was going to stay at your mother's for two weeks, not one as your letter indicates. I'm sure she must have merely "misunderstood," but she did say you told her and that's what she is expecting.

By the way, I do not believe that with joint-custody status you have free rein to make these decisions unilaterally. That is certainly not the intent of the divorce decree.

Enclosed are all of the papers from school. Matthew had to leave his report card at school last week to discuss it with his teachers. He knows he is to bring it to you. I have also enclosed brochures about Williamsburg, which, as you should know, is about an hour from my brother's home. He plans to take the children there for a day trip. My own research tells me it is a wonderful experience for children and will help them learn about American history.

I've already told you I would handle the expenses for this trip. Besides, my family wants the children to come and are happy to help out. I won't ask you to pay your customary share, only to extend your approval as I must confirm the arrangements soon.

Steve

When Alyssa and Matthew were two and six years old their parents separated and were subsequently divorced. Joint legal custody was awarded, and primary residence was given to Lori, with liberal visitation rights for Steve. In the five years since the divorce, conflict has been continuous, and the couple have been back in court multiple times. Disagreements about holidays and summer vacations are common, and last-minute changes by one parent or the other frequently disrupt visiting arrangements. Lori and Steve each believe that the other's home exposes the children to undesirable values and attitudes, and they often talk about these concerns in front of the children. As a consequence, Alyssa and Matthew have become channels for carrying the complaints of their parents back and forth.

In this atmosphere of constant conflict, both parents are fervently convinced they are fighting for the children's well-being. Neither recognizes that Matthew and Alyssa are being pulled apart by the continual arguments or realizes that the worthwhile childhood they are trying to ensure is seriously endangered by their hostility to each other.

When we asked Lori what she hoped to accomplish by sending the above letter, she replied, "Steve had it coming." To her, his overcontrolling behavior justified all her insults. In her anger, she lost her compassionate empathy for the children's needs. Nothing seemed as important as getting back at Steve and proving her independence from his attempts to run her life.

In spite of her reaction, Lori cares a lot about her children's welfare. She works hard at maintaining close relationships with them and wants them to grow up emotionally healthy. Recently, however, eleven-year-old Matthew has formed an alliance with his father, announcing proudly that "We think the same way." The alliance is fast becoming a coalition of father and son against mother, and Matthew has begun to copy his father's judgmental attitude toward Lori. Like his father, he criticizes her alleged disorganization, forgetfulness, irresponsible spending, and volatile emotional displays.

At school Matthew is not doing well and has been getting into fights on the playground. Once a sociable boy and an eager student, he has become subdued and withdrawn in class. He is currently failing in two subjects and is barely maintaining average grades in the others.

Lori is concerned about Alyssa, too. The child often complains of stomach aches and is underactive for a seven-year-old. She takes little interest in the usual play activities of children her age, preferring to stick close to Lori. Overnight visits to her father's home on alternate weekends have become a serious problem and an added source of conflict between the parents. When Matthew is not along, Alyssa often cannot successfully spend the night. As darkness approaches, her distress increases and she telephones her mother asking to come home. Steve's bribes and attempts to persuade her to stay usually fail. In the end, Lori arrives to pick up her daughter, reminding Steve at the door that he is such a poor father his own daughter doesn't want to be with him. Shouting matches marked by degrading, humiliating remarks on both sides generally ensue, as they often have at drop-off and pick-up times.

Matthew and Alyssa, like a third of all children of divorce, are caught in the middle of the animosity between their parents. Many of the usual day-to-day special moments of childhood are marred by Steve's and Lori's anger. What might have been an exciting vacation trip to Williamsburg will probably be spoiled. If Matthew enjoys himself, Lori will be angry. Alyssa, who has not yet mastered separation from her mother well enough to find pleasure in a short visit to her father, will likely be miserable on a long visit to Steve's family. School vacations, report cards, and special school events are all colored by parental accusations and fights over who will attend, who has failed to tell the other, or who is responsible for the good or poor performance of the children.

Each parent demands total loyalty and fails to acknowledge the importance of the other in the children's lives. For the children, everyday life feels fragile, frightening, and unprotected. Rather than offering them permission to love their mother and father equally and to enjoy spending time with each of them, Lori and Steve require, implicitly, that the children choose between them: choose whose side they are on, what to report or not to report, who is the winner and who the loser. The tragedy is, of course, that no one wins, and Matthew and Alyssa are being denied the chance for a happy childhood.

For such children, divorce adds extra burdens to the developmental tasks of growing up. Gaining a sense of competence and self-worth, even in a supportive intact family, is challenging emotional work. Achieving that goal in a conflict-ridden divorced family is a small miracle. The more emotional burdens a child must carry, the more numerous are the psychological tasks to be mastered, and the greater is the risk that he or she will stumble on the road to adulthood. Divorce, in and of itself, is difficult for most children; divorce accompanied by high conflict between parents can demand too much in the way of coping skills to allow children to proceed successfully with their own development. Under these circumstances, the majority will not make it to adulthood unscarred.

Fortunately, unlike the death of a parent or other serious childhood trauma, parental conflict is not incurable, even for parents like Lori and Steve who seem unable to contain their bitterness, even to spare their children pain. Research has shown that couples' ability to co-parent varies widely. The parents of some lucky children naturally evolve cooperative arrangements. Other, potentially high-conflict divorced couples are able to disengage from interaction and avoid direct communication. Their children move back and forth between them in an automated fashion, divided between different worlds. Research has shown that, in the long run, these children fare better than those who live with chronic conflict, but not nearly as well as children whose parents develop a cooperative "co-parenting" relationship.[1]

Most parents have emotional scars left by the failed marriage and must make numerous life adjustments. Every aspect of their lives, from residential arrangements to finances to social and family support systems, must be reorganized. People in the midst of this radical restructuring are usually angry with the person perceived as its cause. Conflict in the first year after divorce is thus normal and predictable.

Usually these feelings lessen by the second year. By the third year, however, parents who still find tempers flaring when talking with each other and who can see no value in each other as parents need help. Such parents *can* learn to manage and control their anger and create a cooperative co-parenting relationship. Achieving such a relationship, however, requires tremendous self-knowledge, acquisition of communication skills, problem-solving ability, and personal sacrifice.

Unfortunately, even parents who recognize their need have few resources to draw on. No schools teach the skills of cooperative parenting, and no one profession is specifically trained in the necessary techniques. Although some mediation services offer training in conflict resolution, it is typically applied to specific issues and oriented to the short term. Family therapists often lack mediation experience and the legal expertise needed to guide parents. Guardians appointed to represent the child's interests in court (guardians *ad litem*) possess legal know-how but are seldom well versed in child development psychopathology or communication techniques.

Mental health professionals who provide individual therapy are likely to hear only one side of the story. While supportive therapy for one parent may ease that person's distress, it may fail to address the underlying dynamics of the conflict. Some therapists' sympathetic stance to their own client may even unwittingly perpetuate or even escalate conflict if the client interprets the support as vindication of his or her position.

Nor is long-term help for parents likely to be found in the

court system. During early stages of separation and divorce, some courts offer classes that teach parents ways to protect children during the divorce process. Although useful in reducing initial tensions, these resources seldom extend to the later period when conflict has become entrenched. A year or two later, the couple may reenter the legal arena, seeking redress for their anger and reassignment of custody, visitation, or child support. The legal system, however, despite the best efforts of court officials, remains adversarial; it is geared more toward declaring winners and losers than toward resolving conflict cooperatively.

Family mediators—the one professional group trained in negotiation, communication, and conflict resolution—may also be consulted at the time of the divorce to help work out differences about custody, visitation, and finances. Although mediation efforts are clearly effective in resolving these issues in the short term, over time they may not facilitate cooperative coparenting. Parents who use mediators at the time of the divorce are no more likely to avoid long-term conflict than those who do not.

Dealing with issues such as a long-distance move by one parent, remarriage, or the changing needs of children as they grow can tax the personal resources even of cooperative parents. Less-than-cooperative parents must face these problems as well as conflicts ranging from occasional disagreements to serious disruptions in the lives of their children.

This book provides those parents and the professionals who work with them with the means to work out the dynamics of their conflicts. The discussion is directed both to parents seeking to educate themselves and find solutions to stressful situations and to the professionals who work with them. Most of all, *Caught in the Middle: Protecting the Children of High-Conflict Divorce* is a book for the benefit of the children. It is the children who are hurt, sometimes every day, who feel helpless and angry, vulnerable and scared. The people they depend on to create a stable world have made them the focus of emotional tension by placing them in the middle of their dispute.

In the first few chapters, therefore, we analyze the nature of postdivorce disputes and help parents and professionals recognize conflict that is not abating. We also explore in detail the ways children of different ages are affected by parental conflict and how they learn to cope with it—often to the detriment of normal developmental processes. Throughout the discussion, we emphasize that it is crucial to identify the conflict dynamics early. Doing so enables parents and professionals to protect children by initiating a parenting plan that minimizes long-term negative consequences and enhances opportunities for the children's unimpeded normal development. Early identification is particularly important in families where a serious form of interparental conflict—parental alienation syndrome—has taken hold. We devote Chapters 6 and 7 to analyzing the syndrome and discussing a model for intervening in such cases.

In Chapters 8 and 9 and in the Appendixes, we offer a conceptual model for parenting: a detailed plan for containing, regulating, and resolving anger. These chapters can guide professionals who are designing parenting plans and helping parents carry them out for the ultimate well-being of their children.

Children of divorce *can* grow into emotionally healthy adults with positive self-esteem and the capacity to form and sustain happy marriages of their own. By listening to the voices of their children, by understanding how they experience the conflict and cope with it, and by learning new strategies for conflict containment and resolution, parents can reframe the divorce experience to make their children the winners.

2

Why Work It Out?

Ask any group of school-age children about divorce and you will quickly sense their uneasy, anxious understanding. Someone in their class, in the neighborhood, or among their relatives lives with divorce. Children know all about moving back and forth between two homes, leaving school assignments at Dad's place or a soccer uniform at Mom's. Even children whose parents are not divorced worry about it. Ordinary arguments between parents can be frightening, arousing fears that divorce might strike their family, too.

Children hate divorce. Listening to the voices of the children who live with it, you hear their pain, disillusionment, and longing. For months, or even years after the decree is final, they continue to hope their parents will stop fighting and work it out—as parents advise children to do when disagreements arise between playmates.

Children of divorce ache inside. Having the two most important people in your life living apart hurts. Even ten years after the divorce, psychologist Judith Wallerstein[1] found that children remained sad, and resentful. They described the family break-up as the most significant event of their childhood, remembering vividly the exact date they were told, who told them, what was said. Like trauma victims, they had flashbacks of the dismantling of their childhood home, of moving-out day, of their first visit to the noncustodial parent. Some used the word cheated—cheated of the experience of growing up in an intact family.

Children do not, then, learn to like divorce, though they learn to live with it. Like any force before which they are helpless, divorce demands an ability to cope with what they cannot change. Although some children are better endowed with this ability than others, for almost all the first two to three years are exceedingly difficult. Not only must they adjust to major changes in their life circumstances, they must also acquire a whole new understanding of what constitutes a "family."

For children, divorce is not a one time event but a continuous process. Over time, it shapes and reshapes their lives and perceptions of the world. The tasks to be mastered and the situations to be coped with change as children mature. Different issues face them as new relationships, remarriages, and long-distance moves further modify the family unit.

Five years after a divorce, children whose parents have successfully created a nurturing, protective environment that allows them to maintain relationships with both Mom and Dad are the fortunate ones. They are likely to be adjusting well psychologically. Ten years later, those who have enjoyed a compassionate, supportive relationship with at least one parent are developing into competent, caring young adults.

Others, deprived of a parent by remarriage or continued parental hostility, are still struggling with the loss. Often other relationships—with peers, teachers, siblings—are troubled. Fifteen years later, having left home and attempting to deal with an intimate relationship of their own, many of these grown-up children of divorce are frightened, and with good reason: They are four times as likely to experience marital failure as children of intact families.[2]

Along the road to adulthood, children of divorce have numerous psychological tasks to master. Wallerstein[3] conceptualizes them as six tasks (as listed below) but points out that children do not accomplish them according to any invariable sequence or orderly timetable.

- Acknowledging the reality of the marital rupture
- Disengaging from parental conflict and distress and resuming customary pursuits
- Resolving losses
- Resolving anger and self-blame
- Accepting the permanence of the divorce
- Achieving realistic hopes for their own relationships

While all children of divorce must find their way through these tasks, some will have a smoother transition than others. Most will stumble along the way and get back up again; others will fall and never recover. Although the tasks are the emotional work of the children, parents who understand the process can lighten the load, lend a supportive hand to shape the course and direction, and help their children come out winners. Professionals who work with them can guide parents and children through these tasks, aiding parents to establish and carry out a co-parenting plan that will give children the best chance of reaching adulthood without the unhealed wounds of divorce.

Who Turns Out Well?

Children can and do weather the stress of divorce. Many grow into competent, happy adults who attain a successful marriage. Although no single factor predetermines how well a particular child will do, recent research into the effects of divorce on children have uncovered seven primary factors. Some of them seem to be the result of simple good luck. Others, however, can be influenced by parents who are willing to educate themselves and to seek help in learning to cooperate with their child's other parent.

Temperament

Considerable research suggests that a child's temperament is one of the best predictors of postdivorce adjustment. With knowledge of a child's temperament, some professionals say, they can almost chart in advance an easy or a difficult course for him or her. Constitutionally resilient children are the lucky ones. Across the board, these easygoing children manage stress well. From early infancy, they display a capacity to soothe and comfort themselves. As babies they easily adjust to a sleeping schedule, accept solid food with eagerness, and navigate each new developmental milestone with minimal difficulty. When told "no," they are less likely to argue or burst into tears than to shift their attention to something else. On the playground, they take rejection in stride, avoid disputes, laugh away disagreements, and get what they want by negotiation instead of fighting. Resilient children have excellent social skills, and adults like and respond to them.

This mellow temperament works very much to their benefit when mastering the tasks of divorce. Being less likely to blame themselves, they move between two homes with greater ease and quickly gain the support of teachers, friends, and other adults.

Although all children can learn some of these skills as they grow, temperament is something a child is born with.[4] The exact opposite of resilient children, difficult children, are often characterized as "reactive." They are active, alert children who demand a great deal of parental time and attention. Their parents walk the floor through much of their infancy. If clothing itches, they won't wear it; it is next to impossible to buckle them into car seats. Every change in life is a major production to be greeted with tears, refusals, and overactivity. It is no surprise that for these children divorce and its accompanying adjustments are likely to provoke tumultuous emotions.

Along with other factors over which parents have no control—gender, age, and family composition—temperament is one element in a complex interaction.

Age

Clearly, there is no "good age" to divorce that will assure children of a positive outcome. Research has shown, however, that the particular issues, level of understanding, and tasks to be mastered vary according to the age at which parents are divorced.[1]

Children under five, for example, hurt the most initially but tend to look the best ten years later. They retain fewer memories of an intact family and integrate with less distress into a single-parent, stepparent, or extended-family household.

Children between the ages of five and twelve, on the other hand, openly grieve, have reunion fantasies, and frequently respond to one parent—or to the entire world—with outright hostility. Because school-age children live in a larger world than preschoolers, divorce influences more aspects of their daily lives. Academic performance almost always suffers for at least the first year after the separation.[6] Peer relationships may be disrupted by changes of residence, long-distance moves, or alternating between parents' households. For children of this age there are more stormy waters to navigate.

Adolescents frequently hurt the most but show it the least. Children twelve and older are highly vulnerable as they begin to deal with their sexuality, prepare to leave home, and learn to form and maintain intimate relationships. It is difficult for them to feel confident about these tasks when their closest models, their parents, have failed at them. Adolescents often report feeling anxious about commitment and intimacy, afraid that they, too, will fail. Some young people become acutely depressed; others develop a pattern of "acting out" at home and school. Still others actively take sides in parents' battles and treat one of them with anger or disdain.

So, while age does not necessarily determine the long-term outcome of divorce, it does shape the course of adjustment and define the tasks to be mastered.

Gender

Parents often ask what difference the sex of the child makes to adjustment after divorce. While research results are somewhat unclear, it is fair to say that being a male or a female does not, in itself, predict a good adult outcome. At first glance, boys seem to fare less well than girls. Early research, however, was somewhat ill defined and mostly conducted in families where the mother was the primary custodial parent. One 1985 national survey, for example, found that boys suffered more upsets in school, social, and personal adjustment than girls did.[5] Wallerstein's long-term study confirmed that finding for the first few years after the divorce.[7]

Yet, when Wallerstein continued her research with the same children, she received some surprises. In the ten-year follow-up study, she found that many of the girls who had shown good adjustment during the early years of the divorce were experiencing significant problems in early adolescence.[7] Thus, gender, in and of itself, does not appear to be protective. The research suggests that boys and girls experience varying degrees of turmoil at different developmental stages.

Another factor, relationship with the same-sexed parent, is also being investigated, and interesting findings are emerging from studies of family composition. Although no firm conclusions can be drawn from the still-scanty evidence, the trend suggests that in nonremarried families, mothers and sons get along less well than mothers and daughters. Upon remarriage, however, sons adjust more quickly than daughters and reap greater benefits from having a stepfather.[8]

Environmental Stability

Divorce typically changes far more than family and interpersonal relationships. It can also mean a new home (or two new homes), perhaps a new school, a geographic move, and, frequently, a lower income. Economic and social stress can dramatically influence the lives of postdivorce families. Two households simply cost more than one. Even with child support payments, the typical woman's income drops 73 percent after a divorce.[9] Because the mother still most often provides the primary home, her reduced income means a changed standard of living for the children. The economics of divorce may dictate that fewer environmental resources—babysitters, nursery schools, after-school care—will be available. In addition, the necessity to return to work, to increase hours of employment, or even to sell the family home often means that the children of a divorced woman must assume more responsibility for themselves and younger siblings. Grandparents, uncles and aunts, and other members of the support network may no longer live nearby or may have been alienated from one parent or the other.

For children, as for adults, stress is cumulative. The more changes in his or her environment a child experiences in a short time, the greater is the risk of long-term adjustment problems. Divorce already involves a loss of family structure. Any additional losses, especially during the first year after the separation, decrease the possibility that children will make a satisfactory adjustment to the divorce.[8] It has been clearly shown that children benefit greatly from remaining in the same house, attending the same school, and retaining a supportive social network.

Psychological Functioning of the Residential Parent

Divorce can greatly affect a person's effectiveness as a parent. During the initial months adults have far-reaching decisions to make about living arrangements, finances, and legal matters related to the divorce. They must face difficult emotional issues and losses. Most parents report that the first year is full of anxiety, sadness, and constant readjustment. Worry about simple survival may overshadow concern about the children. Inadvertently, children may be pushed aside; their needs must wait until other crucial matters are settled. Many divorcing parents, at least temporarily, spend less time with their children and make fewer opportunities to talk with them.

Parent–child interactions are complex and affected by many factors. Parents' levels of stress following a divorce are often directly reflected in their offspring's adjustment; for children react even more strongly to their parents' unhappiness than to their own.[10] If one or both parents are despondent, the children will probably be upset. On the other hand, a mother who desires the divorce is likely to cope fairly well, and her children will probably adjust better than those of a woman who feels that she has been abandoned.[11] Children need increased support at the time of a divorce. Having at least one parent who is able to provide that support increases their capacity to deal with these stresses.

Contact with Both Parents

The most fortunate children are those who can sustain close relationships with both parents after divorce. If, however, these relationships come at too high a cost—because of their parents' intense hostility to each other—they are not so fortunate.[12] Parents who can adopt a cooperative co-parenting style significantly increase the chances that their children will benefit in the long term from maintaining contact with both parents.

On the other hand, the more intense the conflict between the parents, the greater is the likelihood that one parent—usually the father, because he is still most often the nonresidential parent—will drop out of the children's lives altogether. For parents divorced in the 1970s, the dropout rate of fathers was alarming. One nationwide study found that 23 percent of divorced fathers had had no contact with their children during the previous five years.[13] More recent studies have noted a decline in that rate. Most of the children in a recent California study had seen both parents within the past year.[14]

All children need to be loved by both parents. Professionals working with children have long agreed that the loss of a parent to death is the most serious stress a child can sustain. However, when a parent is alive but makes no contact with a child, the risk of serious disturbance is also very high. Not understanding that the problem lies with the adults, children immediately assume that they are at fault or are unlovable.

Mothers and fathers whose cooperative co-parenting allows their children to be loved and nurtured by both of them greatly enhance the chances that their children will cope successfully with the divorce. On the other hand, as parents display increasing levels of conflict and lack of cooperation, children suffer in proportion.

Intensity of Conflict between Parents

The level and intensity of parental conflict is the most potent factor in children's postdivorce adjustment. High conflict between parents is the single best predictor of a poor outcome. Fortunately, it is also one of the factors over which parents have the most control.

Aggression, behavior problems, and depression are frequent early responses to being caught in the middle of continuing animosity between parents.[15] Later in life, too, the children of high-conflict divorce are very likely to suffer serious emotional problems. Ten to fifteen years after a divorce, such children report haunting memories, especially of episodes of physical violence.[7]

Conflict does not, however, need to be physical to be harmful to children. For children, conflict is any situation that places them between their parents or that forces them to choose between them. Being in the middle means anything from hearing one parent belittle the other's values to vicious verbal attacks; from threats of violence to actual violence; from implicit appeals for exclusive loyalty to explicit demands that children side openly with one parent. Whatever form it takes, all conflict hurts. The more intense, pervasive, and open the hostility is, the greater is the damage to the children. And the longer it lasts, the greater the toll it takes.

The majority of divorcing couples battle furiously during the first year. For half of them, according to one study, disputes involve physical violence, even when no abuse took place during the marriage. By the third year, most parents have disengaged and have at least begun to heal emotionally, which reduces the conflict level.[7]

In approximately 25 percent of cases, however, hostility is undiminished and high levels of open conflict continue throughout childhood.[14] Visitation arrangements remain in turmoil, loyalty is constantly demanded, and anger is always present. These are the divorces that produce the high-risk children, for children are more likely to heal if the adults heal. The opportunity to work through the emotional stages of the divorce never comes, because the divorce issues do not go away. The ongoing conflict between their parents is a constant reminder to the children that their right to be loved and cared for by both parents has been irretrievably compromised.

Balancing the Factors

As we have seen, divorce is not a time-limited, single stressful event for children. It is a continuous undermining of the foundations of their safety, emotional security, and day-to-day existence. Divorce is a complex process of coping and healing, restructuring old relationships and building new ones. It is an emotional journey, some of which may be navigated easily and some of which may remain unnegotiable and in turmoil for years to come. Parents who will work to shape the course and directions for their children can greatly increase the likelihood that their children will reach adulthood with their wounds of childhood healed and with the emotional readiness to enter into their own marriages with success. To do so, parents must find a way to balance the seven primary factors we outlined above.

Their success in finding that balance will rest on understanding how the factors interact. For example, one parent's economic difficulties are likely to increase his or her resentment and to lead to heightened tensions. A long-distance move that reduces day-to-day conflict also decreases the time the child can spend with one parent. A reactive, temperamental adolescent capable of long out-of-state visits may refuse to make them, while an easygoing preschooler eager to go will require an adult traveling companion, perhaps making the trip financially unfeasible.

A well-balanced visitation plan that addresses such situations is one of the first requirements of successful coparenting. In many cases, a plan is included in the final divorce decree. Experienced attorneys, knowledgeable judges, courtappointed guardians, or mental health professionals serving as advisers sometimes produce an effective visitation plan. Unfortunately, court dockets are full, judges sometimes rotate among divisions, and attorneys are hired to represent their clients' interests, not the children's. Even mental health workers and guardians *ad litem* may not be skilled at designing workable visitation plans.

Even worse, antagonism between parents is typically highest in the months preceding the final hearing when the plan is being negotiated. At this point it is difficult to distinguish the 75 percent of parents who will subsequently cool off from the 25 percent who will persist in their mutual bitterness. Parents often find themselves saddled with a temporary custody and visitation plan that does not work but that, nonetheless, becomes permanent, by default.

A successful visitation plan, satisfies three essential conditions. First and foremost, a plan will serve the best interests of the children only if it is designed to minimize conflict. Second, it should maximize the time the children spend with both parents as long as both parents (1) know and love the children, (2) are safe guardians for them, and (3) are willing to parent. Finally, the developmental needs of the children must be taken into account. Young children do better with shorter, more frequent visits that gradually lengthen as the child matures.

Parents who are able to co-parent cooperatively can adopt one of the traditional visitation schedules outlined in numerous guides for divorcing parents.[16, 17, 18] These books provide parents and their attorneys with age-appropriate guidelines for designing visitation.

When parents cannot cooperate, however, traditional visitation schedules may be a poor choice because they provide so many opportunities for interparental conflict. They risk thrusting children constantly into the middle of rancorous encounters, and possibly into physical or emotional danger. Visitation between two households requires clear communication, sharing, and frequent contact between the parents. Parents who fight cannot carry out these tasks in a calm atmosphere. For them, reducing conflict must be the primary goal of a visitation plan, the factor that takes precedence over all the others. Regardless of developmental needs, contact with both parents, age, gender, temperament, or economics, children will flounder if conflict is not reduced.

The difficulty is that visitation planning must balance two important but opposing factors: the more visitation, the greater the risk of conflict; the less visitation, the greater the risk of losing the relationship with one parent. High-conflict families attempting to design visitation plans that deal with this knotty dilemma have few resources. In Chapters 4 and 5, we discuss in detail how parents and those working with them can assess a couple's level of conflict and modify traditional visitation schedules to minimize children's exposure to the conflict.

Custody

Until recently, professionals in the legal and mental health fields believed that joint custody was the best postdivorce arrangement for children. It would give them the opportunity to be cared for by both parents and to proceed with their normal development. The majority of states that have adopted a preference for joint legal custody mandate shared decision making in matters of health, religion, education, and the general welfare of the children. The term *preference* means that the court may award joint custody even when one parent objects if it concludes that joint custody is in the best interests of the children. If, however, either parent has been a perpetrator of spouse abuse, child abuse, or neglect, the court will not recommend joint custody.

The legislators who enacted the preference for joint legal custody believed it would be advantageous for the children. They wanted to provide children greater contact with both parents and mothers and fathers with an equal share of the joys and burdens of childrearing. Unfortunately, in many cases the arrangement has not benefited the children. Parents in conflict cannot make joint decisions amicably. The greater the need for parental communication, the greater are the risks that conflict will be expressed through disagreements about the children.[19]

Current research clearly indicates that joint legal custody alone does not assure children a reduction in conflict.[8,20] Recently one psychologist who reviewed the literature on the practice concluded that it should not be awarded if there is a history of "intractable overt hostility" between spouses that has not responded to mediation efforts.[19]

Today the emphasis is shifting to understanding the reasons for ongoing conflict and offering mediation services and training in conflict resolution. Some counties have adopted mandatory mediation requirements for high-conflict parents to address the issues that keep them engaged in conflict. Some states are even contemplating alternatives to custody assignment.

What Do Parents Fight About?

Surprisingly, the most contentious issues are not financial matters but parenting itself. Most ongoing conflict has to do with problems surrounding scheduling, discipline, or arrangements for visits. The following five arenas of conflict pop up again and again in the literature and in parents' complaints about their ex-spouses.

Parenting Skills

Many parents seriously mistrust the other parent's capacity to provide their children adequate supervision, food, medical care, discipline, emotional support, and moral teaching. Disputes may center on one parent's excessive permissiveness or the other's overly strict parenting. A late bedtime or a lost sweater may trigger a conflict. Sometimes the concerns go deeper than childrearing styles and reflect serious fears that the children are in physical or sexual danger in the care of the other parent.

Transition Times

Some children have difficulty moving from one home to the other, even when they are eager to visit the nonresidential parent. Crying, temper tantrums, sleep problems, and general upset prior to or following a visit are common. A parent involved in ongoing disputes with an ex-spouse may be quick to view these responses as signs that the visits are disruptive and should be discontinued.

Time Sharing

Many parents remain embattled over the amount of time the child spends with each of them. Typically one parent wants more time and the other resists.

Details of Visits

Drop-off and pickup times are frequent sources of tension. The child who returns to one parent overtired and late, having left possessions behind, will probably precipitate a parental collision. Lack of communication about changes in plans can be depended upon to unleash accusations of irresponsibility and lack of consideration.

Disparaging Talk

Most couples who remain in conflict object to each other's judgment, lifestyle, and parenting ability. Remarks made in front of the children encourage them to question their other parent's competence.

Rarely do parents carry on their battles completely out of earshot of their children. In fact, research shows that most disputes break out at transition times, often the only time when divorced parents have contact. Consequently, they are likely to deliver their complaints in front of the children. Children hate these moments. If they take sides, they will lose: One of their parents is sure to be angry at them.

Loyalty Binds

We call being caught in the middle in this way a *loyalty bind*. Parents place their children in these predicaments whenever they ask them to take sides, in effect to form a coalition against the other parent. A loyalty bind may be no more than a father's mild encouragement not to comply with the mother's request; or it may be a serious effort to undermine her parental authority. All divorced parents place their children in loyalty binds from time to time. Even the most conscientious people subtly, and often inadvertently, create such a dilemma for their children. It is when a parent fails to take corrective action to minimize such binds that the legacy of damage begins. Children understand that they are part of each parent. They report feeling divided within themselves.

One five-year-old boy, Mark, shared with us the acute distress he felt in a situation demanding that he please one parent or the other. His mother had arrived at his father's home to pick him up. Believing that she was thirty minutes early, his father answered the door and told her to wait half an hour. Instead of returning later, she continued to ring the doorbell and knock on the door, calling Mark to come out. Inside the house his father told the boy to ignore her calls and continue playing. For the next thirty minutes, Mom continued to shout and bang on the door while Dad took Mark to the basement so he would not hear the noise she made.

Children caught in the middle in this way live with constant tension, uneasy alliances, and feelings of fear and intimidation. Most of all, they develop a sense that there is no way they can win. Some children attempt to quiet the storm momentarily by telling both parents what they want to hear. Others shut down communications entirely, hoping that by withdrawing from the fray they can avoid alienating either parent. Still others actively align themselves with one parent as the only solution to their dilemma.

Ultimately, there is no way for children caught in such binds to win. Children of divorce need permission to love both parents and to be loved by both. Asking them to choose sides takes away that permission. By doing so, parents are signaling that their love is contingent, that their own need to win the children's allegiance away from the ex-spouse is more important than the children's feelings. For such children, love and approval come at too high a price.

When a group of researchers asked children what were the most stressful things they experienced about divorce, they ranked the following issues most frequently:[21]

- One parent telling the child the divorce took place because of him or her
- Seeing parents hit each other or hurt each other physically
- Dad telling the child he doesn't like the child to spend time with Mom
- Mom and Dad arguing in front of the child
- Other relatives saying bad things to one of the parents

Least frequent on the children's lists were things that had to do with increased responsibilities, such as taking care of younger siblings or having more household chores. Compared to being caught in the middle, these are mild stressors.

The Long-Term Outcome of High Conflict

We have titled this chapter "Why Work It Out?" The most important reason for working out a contentious relationship is that high conflict has far-reaching negative effects on children. Those who witness intense bitterness between their parents and are caught repeatedly in loyalty binds are at high risk for later emotional disturbance. Parental conflict interrupts many of the critical tasks of psychological development. It changes the nature of the parent–child relationship, creates anxiety and distress, overstimulates and frightens children, weakens parents' protective capacity, and compromises identity formation. Most of all, it leaves children powerless to do anything about it. One twelve-year-old girl, who became suicidal after living with parental enmity for years, said sadly, "As long as I'm alive, this will never stop."

How well children cope with exposure to high-conflict divorce is largely determined by the resources available to them, both internally and externally.[8] Older children with outgoing personalities may disengage from their parents and find support from their peer group, their school, or a trusted adult. Younger children with sensitive temperaments may experience extraordinary anxiety, distress, and regression. Their reactions can range from emotional disengagement to behavioral problems to profound depression. Few children cope really well.

Moreover, serious psychological difficulties in childhood are very likely to persist into adulthood. As adults, these children typically experience problems with intimate relationships, conflict resolution, and self-identity. Growing up without a model for loving relationships between men and women, children of high-conflict divorce are frequently unable to maintain their own marriages successfully. Not having learned the skills of communicating, cooperating, and resolving disputes, they lack problem-solving strategies and tools for handling conflict in an intimate relationship. Even if one or both parents make a successful second marriage, for the children the intensity of the interparental conflict may overshadow later experiences.

These children often face hard struggles in defining their own identity. As they struggle over time to fit into the two polarities represented by their feuding parents, the result is often one of confusion. These children experience a great deal of identity diffusion, liking and accepting some parts of themselves and devaluing other parts.

No parent wishes to impose this kind of lifelong burden on his or her children. Most mothers and fathers express sadness when they recognize the serious toll that conflict takes on their children's happiness and adult adjustment. Yet, many do not know how to stop fighting. Some are so wounded by the marital breakup that they find it impossible to put their own needs aside for the sake of their children. Others are so doubtful of the ability of their former spouse to be an adequate parent that they become harshly critical and even more entrenched in their own style of parenting. Frequently the very issues that led to the breakdown of the marital relationship continue to color the postdivorce relationship.

Divorcing couples often seem to forget that though they no longer choose to live together they must continue to parent together. A cooperative co-parenting relationship is something that divorced parents have to construct. It seldom evolves on its own. Only about a quarter of divorced parents are fortunate enough to find their way to a cooperative arrangement within the first year or two of their separation. Another half of them need to disengage and avoid each other for a period of time. Some of the latter are eventually able to work cooperatively; others need to continue their disengagement to avoid conflict.[14] Finally, the remaining quarter of all divorced parents are completely unable to construct a co-parenting relationship unaided. They remain locked in a bitter struggle that is likely to last throughout the children's formative years.

Yet even these parents are not helpless to stop the conflict. It takes time and effort on both sides to construct a co-parenting arrangement, but the stakes are high. The longer the conflict lasts and the higher its intensity, the greater is the likelihood that the children will be seriously harmed. Having recognized that they are at high risk of remaining in conflict, parents can learn strategies and techniques to reduce children's exposure to the conflict. In subsequent chapters we will help parents gauge the seriousness of their own conflict and structure visitation so as to minimize disputes. We will also present ideas for recognizing the triggers of conflict and, ultimately, finding ways to avoid them by creating and implementing an effective co-parenting plan.

In the next chapter we discuss in detail the effects of conflict on children at various stages of their development—the real reason why parents and the professionals working with them must be determined to "work it out."

3

Understanding Conflict Developmentally

Divorce drastically alters family relationships and, over time, shapes a new internal world for children. It can have different consequences for different children. Some continue to be loved and cared for tenderly by both parents, while others experience nurturance from only one parent. In some cases, children become the witnesses to or the victims of abuse. Still others must live every day with conflict and animosity between their parents.

Interparental conflict can be played out directly between ex-spouses, but all too often children are the focus of disagreements. What does it mean to be the central figure, the main channel of conflict between the two people you love most? How does this affect a child's capacity to love, to gain vital nurturance, and to form long-term relationships later in life?

The answers researchers have found to these questions are not reassuring.[1] They tell us that children caught in high-conflict environments seldom thrive. They are forced to make too many compromises in their own development in valiant efforts to cope with their parents' hostility. Compared to the children of divorces in which conflict is minimal, few of them make it to adulthood with a healthy capacity to form relationships.

29

How Different Ages Cope with Conflict

It is important for parents to understand in some detail how conflict between parents is experienced by children of various ages and levels of maturity. As we explained in general terms in Chapter 2, children cope with divorce itself according to fairly consistent age patterns. In the same way, they handle interparental conflict differently at different ages. Research indicates that these age differences depend principally on an ability to understand the content of arguments (cognitive development), overall maturity, internal resources, and the availability of support systems.[1]

Two- to Three-Year-Olds

Very young children do not understand the content of conflict at all. What they take in and respond to are the feelings expressed. When parents fight in front of them, they feel the heightened emotion, react to the angry tone of the voices, and sense that something is very wrong. Toddlers react to these sensations with confusion, insecurity, clinging behavior, and wide-eyed stares. Some are immobilized, afraid to do anything at all; others respond with panic, crying, temper tantrums, or running aimlessly about. Their primary feeling is fright. The people who keep them safe, who feed and protect them, are out of control, and that feels very scary.

They frequently respond with regression. Young children caught in high conflict look and act less mature than children of similar ages living in conflict-free environments. The safe foundation that enables them to branch out, explore the world, go to preschool, make friends, and learn new skills is eroded. They also worry visibly about their parents, watching them carefully, checking on them frequently, and displaying a fearful reluctance to leave them. When they are visiting with one parent, they will frequently ask about the other parent: "Where is Daddy?" "Where is Mommy?"

Four- to Five-Year-Olds

By the age of four or five, children begin to understnd on a simple level the content of their parents' arguments. They wonder about whether the things they overhear are really true. Some children will ask directly, "Mommy, Daddy says you are mean. Are you?" or "Daddy, Mommy says you don't give her enough money for food." The stronger children check out their concerns; the less emotionally able simply worry silently.

What do they worry about? Children of this age are very concerned about basic needs. They suffer anxiety about their safety and whether there will be enough food to eat. They may worry because Mom or Dad is unhappy and is crying or angry all the time. Often they take on themselves the responsibility for their parents' problems. They feel it is their job to take care of the sorrowing parent, to ask Daddy for more money, or to make Mommy be nice to Daddy. In their own four- or five-year-old way, they understand the problem in concrete terms. They desperately want the fighting and conflict to go away, and, believing that they are all-powerful—as children of this age do—they expect to be able to fix the problem. When they learn over time that they cannot change the situation, they falter. They begin to doubt their own competency and to distrust the world. Emotional disorganization and confusion may set in. At this point, these young children experience the most primitive kind of distress, similar to the two- to three-year-olds' panic, as they lose the confidence that they can control their world.

Six- to Eight-Year-Olds

Children of six to eight are frequently thrust very directly into their parents' disputes. In fact, research suggests that parents actively encourage children of this age to take part in their quarrels. By this age children are likely to become a communication channel, a means for exchanging the complaints of battling parents. Mom may use the children as spies and question them in detail about goings-on at Dad's house. Dad may encourage the children to harass their mother, to complain about things he himself dislikes.

Ninety-five percent of all children of this age who are caught in conflict report witnessing frightening episodes of verbal abuse between their parents.[1] Many say they cannot tell the difference between arguing and physical violence and are acutely upset by all conflict. Others are apprehensive that verbal disputes will erupt into violence and that one or both parents will be hurt. Often they try desperately to stop the fights in order to prevent this scary outcome.

Parents, misunderstanding their intentions, encourage their participation. They urge them to take sides, making them weapons in the battle against each other. Rarely do children of this age have the skill to stay off the battleground, to refuse to spy, or to deliver messages. Most of the time they find themselves unwillingly embroiled in the battle. How do they handle their involvement?

The way children of this age solve their dilemma should come as no suprise. Too unsophisticated to know how to mediate or negotiate disputes between the people they love so much, their solution is simple: Just tell each one what he or she wants to hear. Of course, they have to switch sides regularly to keep up their allegiance to both parents. They may tell Mom they do not want to go to Dad's and then tell Dad they really want to come for an overnight. As both parents scream that they are only reporting what the child said, chances are they are both correct. Still unable to project themselves into the future, children of this age do not imagine the possibility that their parents will compare notes. They simply want relief from the battle and take the most straightforward way to obtain it.

Does this teach children to lie? Yes, in many ways it does. Over time, however, this experience conveys a far more disturbing lesson. It teaches children not to recognize their own true feelings. When they need to polarize themselves and deny their own needs and desires in order to preserve their ties with both parents, children gradually lose their sense of who they are. By adolescence or early adulthood the result may be a lack of a solid sense of identity.

Nine- to Twelve-Year-Olds

By the age of nine, children have gained a much higher level of cognitive skills than younger children. Not only do they understand and grasp the content of their parents' disputes, but they are interested in the ambiguities and in who is right and who is wrong. They are likely to make their own judgments about who and what to believe.

Parents are often surprised to learn how much children of this age know about the issues that are the sources of conflict. Nine- to twelve-year-olds are generally far more knowledgeable about their parents' financial arrangements, pasts, lovers, values, and beliefs than the parents realize. They are intensely curious about the content of conflicts and actively seek information by eavesdropping on telephone calls and snatches of conversations at drop-off and pickup times. They often seek information directly from parents, grandparents, or stepparents.

As they digest this information, they begin to reach their own conclusions. Children of this age typically form very definite opinions about who is right and who is wrong; whom they believe and whom they distrust; and whose side they will take and whose arguments they will reject. Unlike younger children, who struggle to maintain allegiance to both parents, the nine- to twelve-year-old is likely to take sides and to stick to the decision over a long period. In fact, once these children have made their judgments, they become entrenched in them. They seldom change their minds or even actively seek new information that might modify their position.

Moreover, once they have made a firm judgment, they begin to act on it. They may refuse to visit one of their parents, or they may go grudgingly but remain aloof, rude, and uncommunicative. Some children of this age vehemently express their rage at one parent's actions or supposed betrayal of the other. Although they usually reach their conclusions gradually, a single incident may trigger a breach. For example, one girl of twelve had left her diary behind on a visit to her father. Her father, who could hardly stand not knowing what was going on in his daughter's life, unwisely read the diary. Alarmed by its content, he telephoned and confronted her with his knowledge. She was so outraged by this invasion of her privacy that she refused to see him from that day forward.

Adolescence

It is no secret that the adolescent is unpredictable. Some teenagers who make up their minds at ten or eleven never change them and continue to exclude one parent from their lives. But teenagers are independent beings. They may suddenly take a renewed interest and actively seek out a mother or father they have not seen for years. Some parents are surprised to find a child with whom they had long ago lost contact suddenly evidencing interest in them. Parents who earlier felt pushed out of their children's lives by an angry ex-spouse may find that their children no longer align themselves with that parent and are interested in and intrigued by the absent one.

For some parents and children, then, adolescence can be a second chance, an opportunity to heal old wounds and create a new relationship. With their greater ability to act independently, teenagers can make telephone calls or write letters without telling the residential parent. Many like to do it this way. Others will openly announce that they have decided to reestablish the old tie. Sometimes this will not happen until early adulthood, and it may not happen at all. It is a lucky parent who finds his or her adolescent offspring reaching out to forge a new parent–child bond.

Why Is Conflict So Harmful?

As we have emphasized throughout our discussion, the toll exacted by high-conflict divorce is great for children of all ages. Being caught in their parents' pain and anger has detrimental effects on children's happiness and human relationships. Moreover, we are becoming more aware of the long-term dangers that interparental hostility poses for children of divorce. Nothing matters—not custody decisions, visiting arrangements, nor whether the child is a boy or a girl—as much as whether parents can minimize fighting. Over time, parental wars take a greater toll on a child's development than any other single factor in divorce.[3]

Parents may understand that conflict is a serious threat to the child's well-being, now and in the future. Fighting disrupts many of the most vital developmental tasks of childhood and so distorts the child's gradually evolving personality—often for life. Recently, researchers looking at all aspects of the interplay between child development and divorce have uncovered a number of reasons why the influence of parental conflict is so harmful.[2,3]

One of them is that conflict immediately and profoundly weakens the parents' fundamental protective role in the life of their children. Children look to their parents to keep them secure from physical and emotional danger. No one, they believe, can keep them as safe or love them as much as their parents. So when parents are out of control and fighting with each other, that faith is shaken, and the world becomes a very scary place.

As we mentioned earlier, parents' conflict forces children into a middle to which there is no satisfactory alternative. There are only two choices. Either children must take one side and risk losing a parent, or they must chose the middle. For most children, losing a parent is the most dreaded possibility of all. They would rather put themselves in the midst of the battle than lose altogether someone they love. This is why, prior to the age of nine, they generally elect to take the middle. Although they feel acute distress and anxiety much of the time, such feelings are better than being abandoned by a parent.

A third reason why parents' inability to get along is so crucial is that they are a child's first and most important role models. They teach children how to regulate their moods and emotions. They rock children who cannot sleep and bandage skinned knees; they calm temper tantrums and comfort their children when a playmate hurts their feelings. They model how to solve problems, how to restore equilibrium after an upset, and how to manage strong emotions. Imagine, then, what it feels like when suddenly these very same models are unable to manage their own emotions, bursting out constantly with sarcasm and anger and appearing completely out of control. It is very, very frightening to children to witness such intense conflict and to be helpless to stop it. The very people who taught them how to calm and soothe themselves are now modeling the exact opposite behavior.

It is more than confusing—it is scary. And in the long run, not having a good parental model of constructive problem solving leaves children without the skills they will someday need in their own relationships and marriages. This lack of an adequate role model is almost certainly one of the reasons behind the high rate of marital failure among adult children of divorce.[4] More and more research is finding that the major reason for marital breakup is not money or sex or children but how differences are resolved and problems handled.[5]

Moreover, the unique and overwhelming sense of responsibility felt by children caught in the middle of parental conflict easily translates into feelings of guilt. Some children sincerely believe that their parents' fighting is their fault because they are "bad." They feel they are the cause of the problem but are helpless to solve it.

To some children any sort of interaction carries the hope of a reconciliation. At first, they may even enjoy a sense of power of being an important figure in conflict; at least it gives them an opportunity for interaction with their parents. Witnessing conflicts going unresolved over and over, however, brings discouragement and, perhaps, a sense of despair about the possibility of solving life's problems.

The most important of all the reasons why ongoing parental conflict hurts children so much is that it denies them permission to love both their parents. Children who experience cooperative divorce arrangements and have unimpeded permission to love both of their parents even look better three years following the divorce than children caught up in conflict.[6, 9] In several studies the children of conflict appeared depressed, withdrawn, uncommunicative, and aggressive. Boys, in particular, were found to be less socially adept.[6, 7]

How do these children of high-conflict divorce turn out in adolescence and young adulthood? The research results are just beginning to come in, but they are definitely alarming. Janet Johnston and Linda Campbell identified four principal methods children use to deal with unabating parental conflict.[1] The mechanism a particular child adopts is a product of her or his age at the time of separation, gender, temperament, and the strategies for managing stress learned earlier in life.

Maneuvering

Some children become masters at manipulating their parents to get their needs met. Little by little they learn to take care of themselves first and always. Failing to learn empathy or compassion, they become skilled at manipulating others for their own gain.

Equilibrating

Other children become diplomats par excellence. They are always trying desperately to keep everything under control. On the surface they appear composed, well organized, and competent, but they are in fact perpetually anxious. They learn to hide their feelings and to seek safe ways to stay out of parental disputes.

Merging

Children who are not born diplomats often become enmeshed in the contests between their parents. Arrested at the developmental level of the six- to eight-year-olds, they continue to side with the parent they are with at the time. They have split their identities in half and have little individual sense of themselves.

If they have wishes or desires of their own, they are unwilling to express them. In the presence of such children, one feels their sadness and senses a kind of vacancy.

Diffusing

Highly reactive children respond to the constant fighting between their parents the same way they respond to other forms of stress. These children truly do shatter emotionally. Possessing few resources to protect themselves against their parents' warfare, they almost literally fall apart.

No matter which method of coping children adopt, they make an enormous sacrifice in the formation of their own unique identity. Either they must, over and over again, move gracefully between their warring parents without taking sides, or they must mold themselves into some version of what the chosen parent seems to want. It is not within their power to keep their parents from fighting; therefore, they have no choice but to find alternative ways to obtain the love and nurturance they need.

Only since the early 1980s has it become clear to professionals in the divorce field that high conflict is so acutely injurious and that early identification and help for children who are subject to it are essential. Psychologist E. Mavis Hetherington followed one group of children from high-conflict families for six years; these children are now adolescents or young adults. She found that they seemed to develop three different coping strategies and sets of behavior.[6]

She characterized one group of the original research sample of 124 children as coping in "an aggressive and insecure manner." There were three times as many boys as girls in this group, which manifested problems in almost every area of life. Seventy percent of them had no close friends, their grades in school were almost uniformly poor, and their behavior at home was disruptive and impulsive. Not surprisingly, their self-esteem was very low. Hetherington described them as "unhappy, angry, anxious, insecure children." The parents of these children were highly volatile. They carried out incessant verbal and physical assaults on each other, exposing the children to constant emotional upheaval. Neither parent demonstrated any skill at all in conflict resolution or compromise.

The remainder of the children coped far better. They fell into two groups, according to the way they managed anxiety and distress. Both groups maintained good self-esteem, had friends, and were doing at least average academic work. These resourceful children found ways both to manage the pain of the divorce and to reduce the toll of parental conflict.

Hetherington labels the children in one of these groups as "opportunistic" and "competent." Because they used their parents' disagreements for their own gain, they typically had a fairly good relationship with one parent but a poor one with the other. There were as many girls as boys in this group. What they shared was a high level of social skill. Humorous and charming, they were very successful at building relationships with powerful adults and peers. They were not, however, good at maintaining those relationships; interviewers found that within the short interval between interviews they often switched friends.

The other group of successful children Hetherington called "caring-competent." They were less manipulative than the second group, likely to be helpful, and unusually capable of sharing with other children and adults. As you might expect, their friendships were much more enduring. Many of the children in this group had assumed a caretaking role—for siblings or for a physically or emotionally incapable parent—at a very early age. They were more likely to be girls than boys and were similar to the children described by Wallerstein and Blakeslee in their book *Second Chances* as children who grow up too fast.[8]

Many factors interact to determine which of these groups, if any, particular children will fall into. As we have pointed out, some of the factors—the sex of the child and his or her inborn temperament, past experiences of trauma, and age at the time of the separation—are outside the realm of help or change. Other important factors, like visitation planning and parental conflict, can be changed with persistent effort, education, and the use of co-parenting skills. Parents *can* minimize the conflict to which their children are exposed. Even one parent can make a big difference. It takes two to make an argument, and hard as they may be to acquire, it is possible to learn the skills required for *not* fighting. Many of the required techniques have long been taught to couples seeking to reduce fighting within marriages. Only recently have they been brought to bear on the plight of children caught between parents fighting outside rather than inside marriage.

For parents considering the use of such techniques to help their children, the first step must be an honest assessment of their own levels of conflict. In Chapter 4 we present information to help parents begin that process.

4

How to Assess Conflict

Although almost all divorced couples harbor some degree of mutual hostility, especially at first, the ability to refrain from expressing it in front of their children varies widely. Children of divorced parents may witness encounters ranging from mild verbal disagreements that find easy resolution to threats or incidents of physical violence.

Children's psychological adjustment is very directly affected by the amount and intensity of adult anger they experience: The more severe the conflict, the greater the effect. Research shows clearly that children who see their parents fighting display more maladaptive behavior and distress than those who observe no conflict or see only mild anger that is quickly resolved.[1] Not surprisingly, anger involving physical contact frightens children most of all.[2]

No age is immune to the impact of interparental conflict. Children under five, however, are especially upset by adult altercations. Not until they are nine or older do children realize that arguments between adults are not necessarily a threat to themselves. Unfortunately, by this age they are also more likely to have been drawn directly into parental conflict.

Everything possible should be done to protect children from exposure to conflict between their parents. Some parents can respond by being given information in this regard. Upon learning about the risks to their children's emotional well-being, they work to regulate the expression of anger and agree to conduct discussions during times when the children are not present. Other couples simply cannot restrain themselves, in spite of knowing the emotional consequences for their children.

For most parents, the first two years after the divorce are fraught with conflict.[3] By the third year, however, the level of fighting generally subsides. If it does not, it is unlikely to abate on its own. At the outset of the divorce process, however, there are few reliable means to distinguish between parents who will later be able to remain calm in the presence of the children and those who will not.

One way to protect children from witnessing open expressions of anger is to modify traditional visitation schedules. In many cases it is helpful to change the way children move between households, thus reducing face-to-face contacts between feuding parents. Sometimes lessening the frequency of these transitions is the best solution. In extreme cases, it may be necessary to implement supervised visitation or a therapeutic visitation plan.

In general, the more severe the conflict, the more radical the changes need to be. The first step, therefore, for parents and the professionals who may be working with them, is to determine the degree of conflict present. The Conflict Assessment Scale presented in Table 4–1 can help them do so. It is based on two sources of data: (1) the authors' extensive clinical experience with divorcing families and children who experience interparental conflict and (2) the research literature on fighting and violence in divorced and intact families. Although the scale is not a statistically valid or statistically reliable instrument, it may be useful as a guideline in formulating plans for visitation and other matters.

The Conflict Assessment Scale both describes a couple's style of conflict resolution and ability to cooperate and assesses the danger of the environment for children. It describes five levels of conflict—minimal, mild, moderate, moderately severe, and severe—which represent a continuum of conflict rather than distinct categories. For ease of discussion, we have assigned these levels the numbers 1 to 5.

T A B L E 4 – 1
Conflict Assessment Scale

1 Minimal	2 Mild	3 Moderate	4 Moderately Severe	5 Severe
Cooperative parenting	Occasionally berates other parent in front of child	Verbal abuse with no threat or history of physical violence	Child is not directly endangered but parents are endangering to each other	Endangerment by physical or sexual abuse
Ability to separate children's needs from own needs	Occasional verbal quarreling in front of child	Loud quarreling	Threatening violence	Drug or alcohol abuse to point of impairment
Can validate importance of other parent	Questioning child about personal matters in life of other parent	Denigration of other parent	Slamming doors, throwing things	Severe psychological pathology
Can affirm the competency of other parent	Occasional attempts to form a coalition with child against other parent	Threatens to limit access of other parent	Verbally threatening harm or kidnapping	
Conflict is resolved between the adults using only occasional expressions of anger		Threats of litigation	Continual litigation	
Negative emotions quickly brought under control		Ongoing attempts to form a coalition with child against other parent around isolated issues	Attempts to form a permanent or standing coalition with child against other parent (alienation syndrome)	
			Child is experiencing emotional endangerment	

It is important to note that over time the same set of parents is likely to move up and down the scale. Recent research has clearly documented this movement. At the time of the divorce and separation around 50 percent of couples exhibit a high degree of conflict.[4,5] In about half the cases hostility diminishes within two years, especially if the predivorce period was characterized by relative calm.[6] In formulating guidelines for visitation, therefore, it is important to remain flexible. If conflict decreases, restrictive visitation rules may be relaxed, so that the child can enjoy a more spontaneous, less structured relationship with each parent. If interparental animosity intensifies, it will be necessary to modify visitation to protect the child.

In one study of divorcing couples in Marin County, California, 38 percent of the parents were able to communicate "well or very well" on matters relating to their children; 33 percent of the couples reported "satisfactory" communication; and 29 percent described their communication about these issues as "poor" or "very poor." Even so, most of the parents in this study tended to communicate more effectively about their children than about other issues.[4]

If we regard this sample as representative of the larger population, about 38 percent of divorcing couples fall into the minimal and mild categories, about 33 percent into the moderate category, and approximately 29 percent into the moderately severe and severe categories. Another study found that about 14 percent of parents had at some point expressed their mutual antagonism through physical violence.[5]

Divorced couples who fall into categories 1 and 2, minimal and mild, can profitably utilize self-help guidelines; or they may choose to design plans for visitation and other matters in consultation with a therapist or mediator.[7] For the most part, these parents are able to minimize the manifestation of their anger in front of the children. Those in category 3, moderate, may or may not require professional help to manage their conflict. Parents in categories 4 and 5, moderately severe and severe conflict, will probably require ongoing intervention from legal and mental health professionals to help them co-parent.

Category 1: Minimal Conflict

As Table 4–1 indicates, the category of minimal conflict is characterized by both parents' ability to cooperate on issues related to their children, to exercise self-control, and to find effective means to resolve conflict. These traits almost seem to describe a happy couple. Why would two people who can cooperate so well consider divorce? In reality, such seemingly good communication can mask an extreme degree of personal and interpersonal difficulty.

Take, for example, the case of a divorced couple who was mediating a schedule for the residence and visitation of their little boy. The father, Manuel, had such low self-esteem that he felt relieved when his ex-wife, Felicia, remarried. He believed the new stepfather would be a better role model for the boy than he was himself, and he was very amenable to the child's spending less time with him. Felicia, on the other hand, thought her ex-husband was selling himself short and had a great deal to offer their son. She continually encouraged Manuel to remain involved and to maintain a regular visitation schedule. So, although this father's low self-esteem and somewhat passive/aggressive personality style had a good deal to do with the divorce, it did not interfere markedly with his ability to establish a minimally conflicted parental relationship.

Another couple who fall into the minimal conflict group had struggled with difficult external circumstances that strained their marriage beyond its capacity to recover. This young professional couple, Diane and Richard, had three children, the oldest of whom, a boy, had been severely injured in an accident. Diane had left a flourishing career to dedicate herself to giving her son the extra care he required and managing his special rehabilitative routines. As time went on, Diane became increasingly embittered. She complained that her life had been sacrificed to the child's needs and was angry that her husband did not do more to relieve and support her. Richard, however, had taken over the parenting of their two preschool-age children while attempting to sustain his own now-faltering career. Both parents felt personally overwhelmed. Finally, desperate and exhausted, they decided to end their marriage. They hoped that divorce would, somehow, allow them to structure their lives and the lives of their children more satisfactorily. So, in spite of the difficult external problems the family confronted, the divorce was low in conflict, especially from the point of view of the children.

Parents studied by another researcher also found it possible to divorce and subsequently co-parent their children with minimal conflict. This group of parents had realized that the reasons why they had married were no longer valid for them. Many of the couples had wed very young. As they grew older, they had gradually defined themselves in ways that were no longer mutually compatible. Even though there was little or no animosity between the spouses, they found that they could not help each other attain their new goals.[4]

Category 2: Mild Conflict

The defining feature of category 2, mild conflict, is its occasional nature, as shown in Table 4–1. Parents in this category sometimes quarrel or berate each other in front of the children. For example, the mother may attempt to pry information about the father from the children, or the father may attempt to form a short-term coalition with them against the mother.

Mild conflict is distinguished from category 3, moderate conflict, by its lack of intensity and duration. Couples in mild conflict periodically disagree, and certain issues perhaps remain unresolved. Still, these parents do not conduct continual power struggles over decisions related to the children. Most of the time they are able to co-parent effectively.

This category of conflict is illustrated by Cathy and Doug, who attempted unsuccessfully to mediate a residence and visitation arrangement at the time of their separation. Initially, Doug was deeply injured because Cathy wanted the divorce, and he was determined to get revenge. He resolved that she was "not going to see a penny in the settlement" and vowed not to make his child-support payments. Totally blind-sighted by his hurt feelings, he lost track of the protection he owed his school-age son. He even quit his job and remained unemployed for a number of months, thus temporarily attaining his goal of not making support payments.

Within two years, however, both Cathy and Doug had remarried, and they were able to attend their son's school events together. They are typical of a fair percentage of families, which look intensely conflicted at the point of separation but over time experience a considerable diminution of anger.

Another couple in the mild conflict category are Nancy and Jim. Nancy was very supportive of Jim's efforts as a divorced father until, in her words, "he chose to live in sin." When Jim moved in with Debbie, his new girlfriend, Nancy's sense of morality was outraged. Her refusal even to mention Debbie, whom the two children referred to as their stepmother, created a good deal of tension for them. Nonetheless, conflict between the parents was largely confined to this one area, and they maintained a mostly successful co-parenting relationship.

Parents who fit the minimal and mild conflict categories can usually follow customary guidelines for visitation and manage their differences with minimal outside intervention and support. Unlike parents in the next three categories, they are able to minimize the expression of their conflict and protect children from exposure to it.

Category 3: Moderate Conflict

The moderate level of conflict in Table 4–1, category 3, includes people who function effectively as parents on one level. Individually, they promote positive ideals for their children, but when they attempt to work together, power struggles and almost-constant conflict ensue. All too often the children hear their parents exchanging verbal abuse, mutual insults, and threats of litigation. What is worse, conflict in this group fails to abate over time. It may even intensify as both parents become further entrenched in the roles they play with the children and with each other.

One such divorced couple, Sarah and Carl, became embroiled in a bitter conflict over the safety of Carl, Jr. Carl allowed his ten-year-old son to walk the two blocks to the corner grocery store unsupervised, as other children his age did in the neighborhood. Sarah, who lived in a different part of town, was convinced the trip put her son in danger. She was determined to keep this from happening and instructed the boy that he was not to go to the grocery store alone while at his father's. On the very next visit, Carl asked his son to run to the store to pick up a few household items. The child did not know which way to turn, or whom to obey. He was in a classic loyalty bind. To please one parent was to displease the other.

What is significant about these parents, and others like them, is that each of them, though competent and caring, is so determined to win the power struggle that they cannot work together, even for the sake of their children. Friends, co-workers, and community members testify to the compassion and intelligence exhibited in every other aspect of their personal and professional lives. Yet, when they are together, they battle constantly for supremacy and fail to protect their children from the effects of their mutual hostility.

Another example of moderately conflicted parents is Janet and Frank, the parents of five-year-old Mark, whose unhappy predicament was described in Chapter 2. When his mother arrived to pick him up half an hour before his father expected her, Dad refused to let Mark leave. Frank slammed the door in Janet's face and took Mark to the basement, while his mother pounded on the door and shouted to the boy to come out. Inside the house, torn between his parents, Mark became almost hysterical. Although not in physical danger, he was in the middle of a fierce combat and the worst kind of loyalty bind.

Category 4: Moderately Severe Conflict

Moderately severe conflict subsumes all high-conflict situations short of those that involve direct endangerment to a child through physical and sexual abuse. Category 4 extends to living in a violent environment in which parents batter each other verbally and threaten violence, litigation, and even kidnapping.

It also includes the parental alienation syndrome, in which one parent actively attempts to exclude the other parent from the children's lives. Continually putting the children into loyalty binds, these parents force them—with implicit threats and subtle inducements—to choose one parent and reject the other. This process is closely akin to brainwashing and, over time, may cause children to refuse visitation or even all contact with the targeted parent. This form of abuse is so injurious to children's development that we devote two chapters, Chapters 6 and 7, to describing in detail how it occurs and how it can be treated.

Moderately severe conflict defines an environment that is psychologically abusive to children. Every day, they live with the fear that violence will erupt that will harm one or both parents or themselves. They learn to know the bitterness of continual litigation. When parents are constantly tense and focused negatively on each other, children cannot thrive.

Category 5: Severe Conflict

Severe conflict represents an environment that is an immediate and direct threat to children's emotional and physical safety. Children in these families are at exceedingly high risk of damage from parental physical or sexual abuse, drug or alcohol abuse, and/or severe psychological pathology. Safeguards are essential to protect such children.

There is a wide variability of response to treatment in people manifesting any of the above problems. For certain constellations of behavioral difficulties, the prognosis is very poor.[8] For others, it is only guardedly optimistic. Insuring that children will be safe during visits to such parents is mandatory. Safeguards can be relaxed only after the affected parent has completed a comprehensive treatment program and an adequate period of time has elapsed to insure that the behavior will not recur. Even then, some say, the risk is too grave.

Most divorced parents, once their level of interparental conflict has been established, can begin to work out a suitable visitation plan for their children. In the next chapter, therefore, we discuss in some detail the recent research on visitation for children of different ages and describe the process of designing visitation plans for high-conflict parents.

5

Normal Visitation versus Conflict Visitation

Arranging for their children's residence and visitation is one of the first joint decisions a couple must make as divorcing parents. If they cannot reach agreement by themselves or with the assistance of attorneys, mediators, or mental health professionals, the court will make the decision for them. The typical final divorce decree specifies the type of legal custody (joint or sole), the physical custody of the children (where they will live), and a visitation schedule for the nonresidential parent.

Nowadays parents and judges alike recognize the necessity of tailoring these arrangements to the specific circumstances of the family. Experience has shown that the design of a residence and visitation plan must take into consideration four principal factors:

- The ages and developmental needs of the children
- The parenting capacity of each parent
- Whether endangerment or abuse is likely when the children are in the care of either parent
- The socioemotional environment each parent will create

Courts and mental health professionals have assumed that the more contact children have with both their parents, the better off they will be in the long run. Research has generally supported this notion, with one significant exception: when the parents are in high conflict.[1,2] In fact, recent research has found that frequent visitation can exacerbate the conflict and place the children into the midst of the battles more often.[3,4] The degree of hostility between the parents is emerging as a decisive factor in children's postdivorce adjustment.

At present, however, parents, mental health professionals, and judges have no tool for measuring conflict and designing visitation to minimize its impact on children. In an earlier work, *Children of Divorce,* we offered a set of guidelines for planning visitation based on the developmental needs of children.[5] These guidelines, although appropriate for parents at minimal or mild levels of conflict, need to be adjusted to varying degrees for parents in the moderate, moderately severe, or severe categories on the Conflict Assessment Scale presented in Table 4–1. The reason for this recommendation is simple: Frequent visitation aggravates interparental conflict and places children in the middle of the battlefield.

We have therefore described the modifications recommended for each age group and for each level of family conflict. The modified guidelines for visitation are presented in Tables 5–1 through 5–5. To use the tables, first identify the parents' level of conflict on the Conflict Assessment Scale. Then consult the appropriate table for each child's age group and find the modified guidelines in the column corresponding to the identified level of conflict.

Minimal and Mild Conflict

Parents falling into the minimal and mild categories of conflict can usually co-parent effectively by using the traditional visitation guidelines suited to their children's developmental ages.

Moderate Conflict

Parents who fall in the category of moderate levels of conflict frequently function well as individual parents but are prone to

T A B L E   5 - 1
Infancy to Two & One-Half Years

	Level of Conflict			
Minimal	Mild	Moderate	Moderately Severe	Severe
Select primary residence based on caretaking history.	Nonresidential parent has short, frequent visits—daily depending on availability and caretaking history.	Daily visits possible if in neutral environment that infant is comfortable in (i.e., day care, trusted friend or relative, supervision service).	No visits at home. Visits twice a week in a supervised environment.	Supervised or therapeutic visitation only.
	If dual primary residence, parents share daytime caretaking and establish one nighttime caretaker. Overnights are not recommended.	Two home visits per week possible provided conflictual environment can be neutralized. If parents cannot adhere to minimal verbal exchange, neutral visiting environment is mandatory.	Assessment mandatory before unsupervised visitation possible. Full assessment to consider each parent's capacity (1) for impulse control; (2) to change problem-solving style; (3) to empathize with child; (4) to create and maintain a safe environment.	

T A B L E 5 - 2
Two & One-Half to Five Years

	Level of Conflict			
Minimal	Mild	Moderate	Moderately Severe	Severe
Time initially distributed in proportion to parent's direct caretaking prior to divorce.		Minimize transitions. Eliminate midweek visit.	Supervised visits only until full assessment of parents and child obtained.	Supervised or therapeutic visitation only.
May introduce longer visitation periods for child gradually throughout this stage to a maximum of a split week.		Move toward one lengthier visit per week—2 days/1 overnight initially, moving to 3 days/2 overnights toward the end of this stage.	Frequency of supervised visitation determined on a case-by-case basis, taking into account the child's feelings (i.e., child is not expressing fear of visitation).	
Implement overnights for child—1 per week initially, extend to a maximum of 3 per week toward the end of this stage.		Use neutral transition places whenever possible.	Full assessment to consider each parent's capacity (1) for impulse control; (2) to change problem-solving style; (3) to empathize with child; (4) to create and maintain a safe environment.	
Long-weekend–short-weekend concept, preferably including a weekday visit, is a possibility if one parent works full time during the week and the other does not.				

T A B L E 5 - 3
Six to Eight Years

	Level of Conflict				
Minimal	Mild	Moderate	Moderately Severe	Severe
Many children still require a home base. Child visits from 1 to 3 days weekly with nonresidential parent. OR Alternating half weeks at each parent's home if consistent contact with community, peer group, school, and extracurricular activities can be maintained. Child could have multiple overnights. Full week at each parent's home can be phased in toward older end of this stage.		Minimize transitions. Use neutral transition places—school, activities, day care. Distribute visitation into one time block per week.	Supervised visits only until full assessment of parents and child obtained. Frequency of supervised visitation determined on a case-by-case basis, taking into account the child's feelings (i.e., child is not expressing fear of visitation). Full assessment to consider each parent's capacity (1) for impulse control; (2) to change problem-solving style; (3) to empathize with child; (4) to create and maintain a safe environment.	Supervised or therapeutic visitation only.

T A B L E 5 - 4
Nine to Twelve Years

	Level of Conflict			
Minimal	Mild	Moderate	Moderately Severe	Severe
One home base with specific evenings, weekends, and activities at the other home scheduled for regularity and predictability OR		Minimize transitions. Distribute visitation into one longer block—split week, alternating weeks, or up to 2 weeks in each residence.	Supervised visits only until full assessment of parents and child obtained.	Therapeutic visitation only.
Equal basis with each parent is possible, up to 2 weeks in each residence.		Transition handled by child (bike or public transportation), or an agreed-upon neutral place (school, activity, or sitter) is selected.	Frequency of supervised visitation determined on a case-by-case basis taking into account the child's feelings (i.e., child is not expressing fear of visitation).	
Maintain accessibility to school, peers, and extracurricular and community involvements from both homes.		No nesting.	Full assessment to consider each parent's capacity (1) for impulse control; (2) to change problem-solving style; (3) to empathize with child; (4) to create and maintain a safe environment.	
"Nesting": Both parents' moving in and out of same residence is another possibility.		Therapy considered if child refusing visitation or strongly taking sides.		
Presuming close relationship, summers may be split 50-50, approximately 4 to 6 weeks in one block.				

T A B L E   5 – 5
Thirteen to Eighteen Years

	Level of Conflict			
Minimal	Mild	Moderate	Moderately Severe	Severe
One home base with specific evenings, weekends, and activities at the other home scheduled for regularity and predictability OR Equal basis with each parent is possible up to 2 weeks in each residence OR "Nesting": both parents moving in and out of same residence is another possibility. Establish "permanent schedule" with some flexibility built in. Adolescent input essential; adolescent cannot be forced into schedule he or she had no involvement in creating. Maintain child's accessibility to school, peers, and extracurricular and community involvements from both homes.		Minimize transitions. Distribute into one longer block—split week, alternating weeks, or up to 2 weeks in each residence. Transition handled by child (bike, car, or public transportation), or an agreed-upon neutral place (school or activity) is selected. No nesting. Therapy considered if child refusing visitation or strongly taking sides.	Supervised visits only until full assessment of parents and adolescent obtained with following exception: When adolescent is aware of endangering situation, is capable of leaving independently, and is expressing a desire for unsupervised visitation, such visitation should be given consideration. Frequency of visitation determined on a case-by-case basis taking into account the adolescent's feelings. Full assessment to consider each parent's capacity (1) for impulse control; (2) to change problem-solving style; (3) to empathize with adolescent; (4) to create and maintain a safe environment.	Therapeutic visitation only.

fight and argue when they are face to face. Children from these families, therefore, benefit from transitions especially designed to minimize contact between the parents. Younger school-age children can be picked up at school, the day care center, or a babysitter's house. Many older children can take responsibility for getting back and forth on their own. Preschoolers and infants, however, pose greater difficulties. In a few cities there are now drop-off and pickup centers for busy or warring parents. Transferring children in public places like restaurants, hotel lobbies, or shopping malls can also reduce the likelihood of interparental conflict. Sometimes relatives and friends who do not take the side of one parent against the other can serve as intermediaries. Whatever the arrangement, the less parents at the moderate level of conflict see of each other, the better it is for the children.

Parents in moderate conflict who choose or are awarded joint legal custody have many opportunities for disagreement. After the first painful year or two, some parents settle into milder patterns of conflict. Others, however, continue to argue over the numerous joint decisions that must be made under this custody arrangement—decisions about the children's education, health care, religious training, and extracurricular activities. If parents come to an impasse over these matters, a mediator or arbitrator may be appointed to assist them. More frequently, however, they wind up back in court. In fact, couples awarded joint custody over the objections of one or both parties reinitiate litigation more often than any other group of divorced parents. Therefore, joint custody does not, in and of itself, keep the conflict contained.

An alternative that has been found tenable for some couples is called *demarcated joint custody*. This is not a legal term, nor even a concept familiar to many legal and mental health professionals. It means that each parent has sole decision-making power in specific areas. One parent, for example, may make all decisions relative to the children's education, while the other is responsible for extracurricular and religious activities. Such an arrangement can take advantage of parents' individual strengths and interests.

Most of all, parents in moderate conflict need a very well-structured and detailed visitation agreement. For the children's sake, it should minimize the number of transitions they must make each week, whenever possible combining shorter visits into longer ones. Because of school and work schedules, this may mean that children will spend fewer hours with one parent than with the other. In any case, time-sharing must be precisely specified, leaving minimal leeway for changes in drop-off and pickup times. If a parent misses a drop-off or pickup time, the visit is forfeited. Arrangements for all holidays and school vacations, as well as travel for vacations, must be clearly spelled out. Trading days or holidays is not allowed, except when arranged through a mediator or arranged in writing signed by both parents.

The agreement might need to restrict joint attendance at school functions, recitals, or sporting events, dividing them fairly between the parents ahead of time. Even seemingly trivial issues such as the movement of clothing, school supplies, and toys should be clearly defined. How to manage children's telephone calls to the other parent during visits is a critical issue. One often-successful arrangement limits strictly the number of calls and the times calls can be made from parents to children, while providing for open access of children to parents.

The point to keep in mind is that any issue not clearly spelled out can become fertile ground for disputes. Although some parents mourn the loss of spontaneity in their relations with their children, such highly structured arrangements can insulate children from conflict while providing them with the maximum amount of time in each household. In Appendix A we provide a sample agreement that parents or professionals can use as a model for designing a visitation or co-parenting plan of their own.

As they redefine their lives and locate new support systems, many moderate-conflict parents find their mutual hostility dissipating. If it does not do so after a year or two, however, they should consult a parenting coordinator, as explained more fully in Chapters 6 and 7.

Moderately Severe Conflict

Moderately severe conflict defines an environment that is psychologically abusive to children. It forces them to live with continual litigation and with the constant fear that they or their parents may fall victim to physical violence.

Because of the direct threat to these children's emotional and physical well-being, all families entrenched in moderately severe conflict should be thoroughly evaluated before a visitation plan is negotiated. Assessment must be made of one or both parents' abilities in

- Impulse control
- Changing problem-solving style
- Empathizing with the children
- Creating and maintaining a safe environment

Such an evaluation should be undertaken only by a professional or a professional team with specific training and experience in working with parents of this kind. Even the best-qualified therapists and mediators find it difficult to predict which of the parents' verbal threats of violence or kidnapping will escalate into actual behavior. If there is any doubt, the children's safety must take precedence over the parents' visitation rights.

During the assessment phase, supervised visitation is recommended if one parent exhibits behavior that may endanger the children. If both parents display such behavior, it may be necessary to place the children outside the home until the assessment is complete. Only when the risk of danger is judged to be high, however, should such a drastic disruption of the parent–child relationship be considered.

When the evaluation is complete, the evaluator or the evaluation team should formulate a detailed and individualized co-parenting plan in keeping with their findings. It may be necessary to limit children's visits to one parent or to arrange for supervised visitation. Plans that limit visits to one of the parents sometimes provide for longer and/or more frequent visits as that parent improves his or her ability to create a safe setting that is less subject to conflict.

The evaluator or evaluation team will need to consider carefully any evidence of two highly dangerous conditions for children that are sometimes present in moderately severe conflict. The first, the parental alienation syndrome, is a complex interplay of family dynamics. We devote Chapters 6 and 7 to a comprehensive discussion of this syndrome and a proposed intervention model for dealing with it.

The second situation, spouse abuse, also has grave consequences for children, even if the children are not currently its victims. One survey of research in this field found that half of the children who had observed marital violence became involved in abusive relationships later in life. Most of the girls became victims of abuse, and all of the boys became perpetrators.[6]

In any given case, it is difficult to predict whether spouse abuse will turn into physical abuse of the children. One study found that 45 percent of the men who abused their wives also eventually began abusing their children.[7] Research on wives battering husbands is beginning to emerge as well. Robert Geffner, President of the Family Violence and Sexual Assault Institute, estimates that men are the victims in 5 to 10 percent of domestic fights.[8] Because of underreporting by relatives reluctant to press charges, statistics on all kinds of family violence may be unreliable.

Even so, children exposed to any level of marital violence should be carefully evaluated. Signs of anxiety or fear should be taken very seriously. Children who have witnessed spouse battering are sometimes too frightened to visit the battering parent.

Until the children's safety can be ensured, supervised visits are the only alternative. As the first step toward rehabilitation, battering parents must take full responsibility for their behavior. Justifying it by claiming that the other parent deserved or provoked the attack is not a healthy model of conflict resolution. Moreover, mothers or fathers who have resorted to physical violence need to tell children clearly that it is not an appropriate method of solving problems and that they are working at finding other ways to express their anger.

Movement away from supervised visitation must always be cautious and very gradual. Many explosive parents can control their anger when not faced with the day-to-day frustrations and responsibilities of parenting. A cessation of violence during supervised visitation is no guarantee that violence will not break out again when there is no supervision. The younger the children, the more guarded the supervisor must be, for preschoolers cannot or may not accurately report what has occurred during a visit. Any sign of anxiety or fear on the part of the children must be taken seriously. A once-traumatized child can be retraumatized easily.

Severe Conflict

As defined in the preceding chapter, severe conflict creates an environment that puts a child at immediate risk of suffering physical or sexual abuse or being exposed to a parent's substance abuse or serious psychological pathology. For children of any age who have parents in the severe-conflict category, supervised visitation is the only recommended alternative.

For children more than nine years old, according to psychologists Johnston and Campbell, supervised visitation is not enough.[2] It needs to be combined with some type of therapeutic intervention. They base their recommendation on evidence that school-age children often take sides in intense parental conflicts and withdraw from the parent they hold responsible. Many of these children also exhibit enhanced levels of aggressiveness and behavioral problems in other parts of their lives. Consequently, such children need more than safekeeping; they need help detaching themselves from their parents' aggressive role model and reconstituting a relationship with the parent they blame for the problem.

Supervised visitation and therapeutic visitation are different techniques. During supervised visits, the parent and child (or children) are usually observed by a paraprofessional or staff person in a hospital setting. Sometimes the person sits in a different room and monitors the visit through a microphone or one-way mirror; at other times the staff member is in the same room with the parent and the child. His or her principal function is to ensure the child's safety. In therapeutic visitation, on the other hand, psychotherapy takes place during the visit, as an experienced mental health professional intervenes actively to effect change in the parent–child relationship.

In all cases of severe conflict, it is essential that a mental health professional be involved with the family on an ongoing basis. Not only will an initial evaluation, similar to that recommended for moderately severe conflict, be necessary but ongoing visitation planning will be an important issue. Many parents in this category will not be ready to move away from supervised visitation for a long time, and the change must be planned with great care, so that the plan gives the safety of the children the highest priority. A parent who has been abusive, who has serious impulse-control problems, or who has a history of chemical dependency is a high-risk parent. The success rate of therapeutic interventions with these parents is low, and the recidivism rate is high.[9] Professionals involved with severe-conflict families must be highly skilled and knowledgeable about the devastating effects of high conflict on children and may need to testify in court. When all efforts to remedy the conflict and its underlying causes fail, the court may elect to terminate parental rights.

Nonetheless, change, though painful and difficult, is possible for some of these families. One successful mediation project involved eighty high-conflict families that had suffered an incident of physical aggression, on the average, once a month. Two to three years after mediation, violent episodes had almost completely ceased.[4]

Professionals working with families in severe conflict frequently have to weigh the positive value of a continued relationship with a high-risk parent against the negative impact of complete loss of the parent. Are children hurt more by continued visitation with a parent who has injured them or by losing that parent? There is no clear answer in every case. At the very least, the decision to terminate visitation should be reached

only after one to two years of intervention by skilled professionals. If a parent exhibits no change of attitude or behavior
by then, elimination of visitation is usually the wisest course—
especially if the child displays anxiety, refusal, or acting-out
behavior in connection with the visits and has no history of
close attachment to the parent.

There are other ways children of high-conflict divorce can
lose a parent. One of the most destructive for the child's well-
being and future development is parental alienation, which we
discuss in detail in the next two chapters.

6

Identifying and Understanding Parental Alienation

For children, the one tragic effect of divorce can be the complete loss of a mother or father. Sometimes a parent can no longer bear the strain of sustained combat with an ex-spouse and simply walks out of the children's lives. Or a child, weary of being constantly in the middle of parental wars, sees severing contact with one parent as the only escape. Finally, in what has come to be known as "parental alienation syndrome," one parent encourages a child to reject the other parent.[1]

Unfortunately, many parents and professionals, viewing parental alienation as a rough equivalent of "brainwashing," use the term to pin blame solely on one parent for a child's rejection of the other. Parent–child relations, however, are seldom so simple. Rejection of a parent is a complex process to which both children and parents contribute according to their individual tolerance for conflict. For example, a sensitive child at a particularly vulnerable age may react to messages of conflict between parents by refusing to visit the nonresidential parent; a hardier child may have no trouble dealing with both parents in spite of repeated exposure to their heated encounters. Parents, too, vary in their tolerance. What drives one to withdraw from the parental role may energize another into greater rage, renewed litigation, or an attempt to undermine the children's relationship with the ex-spouse.

In considering the parental alienation syndrome, it is important to keep in mind that it is defined by no agreed-upon set of criteria; nor has scientific research documented its existence or completely described its clinical manifestations.

Nonetheless, parental alienation is very real. It occurs when one parent convinces the children that the other parent is not trustworthy, lovable, or caring—in short, not a good parent. This persuasion may be consciously malicious and intended to destroy the children's relationship with the other parent. Or it may take a more insidious, even unconscious form arising from the personality issues as yet unresolved in the childhood of one parent. Although not an immediate danger for a child, over time parental alienation carries very high risks: it can seriously distort a child's developing personality and subsequent life adjustment. The sooner it is identified and appropriate interventions are implemented, the better are the child's chances of avoiding its worst long-term effects.

In this chapter, we describe the main features of the alienation syndrome and explore the complex interplay of the individual and situational dynamics that bring it about. In Chapter 7, we present a comprehensive intervention model for legal and mental health professionals to use in treating the syndrome.

Even for the well-trained professional, the first step, recognition of the parental alienation syndrome, is difficult. Divorced parents frequently express doubts about their ex-spouse's childrearing ability, home environment, and judgment. Several key features of the syndrome, however, can help to differentiate it from the usual sort of interparental complaints.

One such feature is the tendency of alienating parents to discuss concerns about parenting matters better left to the adults with the children themselves. Instead of taking their complaints to the ex-spouse, a therapist, or another responsible adult—where they might be resolved—alienating parents express them directly to the children. Implicitly or explicitly, the criticisms become reasons why the children should not spend time with the other parent.

In most cases of parental alienation the child has a stronger attachment—even if an unhealthy one—to the alienating parent than to the targeted parent. The alienating parent uses this emotional tie to gain an advantage. Even when there is no explicit threat, the child senses that the alienating parent's continued nurturance is contingent upon expressions of loyalty and agreement. Deprived of the opportunity to form his or her own opinion, the child learns that an alliance with the alienating parent is the only way to feel loved and protected.

Another identifying characteristic of the alienating parent is the sincere belief that the children will benefit by being raised without interference from the other parent. Such a parent often cannot cite even one reason why children need close relationships with both parents. When Sarah, the mother of a nine-year-old girl, was asked to name all her objections to visits between the girl and her father, she listed fifteen areas of varying importance. After discussing them, the therapist asked whether she would consent to visits once these fifteen obstacles had been cleared away. Sarah was speechless. She could not say "yes," for she realized that when all her complaints had been remedied, she would no longer have a legitimate reason to refuse visitation. Ultimately, visits with the father were simply unacceptable under any circumstances.

This is a typical reaction of alienating parents. Even when assured that children will be kept safe through supervised visitation or therapeutic intervention, they are unwilling to allow visits. Their main agenda is not to solve the problem but to break up the relationship between the children and the other parent.

Another sign of parental alienation is children's resistance to visiting one parent. When children say they are afraid to visit, sometimes it may be hard to tell whether they are actually in danger or whether they have been subtly convinced that they will be harmed. In some cases, children's accounts of an incident make it difficult for a parent to get an accurate idea of what actually happened. A child may describe something that occurred in alarming or colorful terms or may leave out some of the facts, leading the listening parent to jump to the most dire conclusions. Perhaps the nonresidential parent used poor judgment and handled a situation badly but did not place the child in any real danger. In the heat of interparental conflict, a minor instance of bad judgment can easily balloon into a full-scale scenario of abuse or negligence. Finally, it must be recognized that vengeful parents do sometimes intentionally stretch the truth or lie outright.

Usually, however, a parent who is legitimately concerned about his or her children's safety in the other parent's home can be distinguished from an alienating parent. He or she is generally willing to accept therapeutic help so that visits can continue. A parent who is truly alienating, like Sarah, is not interested in repairing or alleviating the problem.

In all cases, it is critical to sort out real abuse from alleged abuse, for a child living in or visiting an abusive household is at extremely high risk for serious long-term emotional disturbance. All situations in which abuse is alleged must be quickly evaluated by competent mental health professionals while measures to protect the children are immediately put in place. In all fifty states, suspected cases of child abuse must also be reported to local social services and fully investigated.

More allegations of physical and sexual abuse are made at the time of separation and divorce than at any other period. Research indicates that about half of them appear to be well founded. In one review of 9,000 disputes over custody and visitation, investigators discovered 169 allegations (1.5 percent) of sexual abuse. They determined that abuse probably did occur in 50 percent of those cases and did not in 27 percent; they could reach no firm conclusions about the remaining 23 percent.[2] A child custody evaluator in the Denver area came to similar conclusions. Investigating the approximately one-fourth of disputed custody cases involving allegations of abuse convinced her that the accusations were justified in about half the cases.[3]

During the evaluation period for abuse, the child must be protected and reassured in case the allegations turn out to be true. On the other hand, suspension of visitation may be destructive to the child's relationship with the parent and unfair to both, especially in a suspected case of parental alienation.

The strongly recommended safeguard for the investigatory period is, therefore, supervised visitation as described in Chapter 5 for cases classified as severe on the Conflict Assessment Scale. Once the evaluation is complete, visitation can be restructured according to the findings.

Why Is Early Recognition So Crucial?

Although parental alienation often starts long before the divorce, it may first surface and become recognizable when visitation arrangements are being worked out. Sometimes one parent uses the legal system to delay, postpone, and draw out the litigation while instilling in the children worries about being unsafe when visiting the other parent. An alienating parent may agree to a visitation schedule only to undermine it once it has been adopted. He or she frequently denies exerting any influence, claiming that the children are unwilling to make the agreed-upon visits and must be listened to. More court dates are set and reset; more hearings are scheduled and postponed. The ongoing legal proceedings become an asset for the alienating parent, a way to an indefinite delay in reaching a conclusion about visitation imposed by anyone but themselves. The delay also allows the alienating parent more time and opportunity to persuade the children that visiting the other parent is unsafe and unenjoyable and is not something that they have to do.

The more time that is spent identifying and intervening in the syndrome, the more powerful and effective the alienation may become. Early recognition and intervention are thus critical. The longer this syndrome is allowed to progress, the more difficult it is for the legal system or the mental health professional to intervene effectively to stop it. A parent who has fully persuaded the children that visitation is undesirable or dangerous can impede the efforts of even the best professionals to change that point of view. Once children are "programmed"—as measured by their refusal to visit one parent—deprogramming them without harming them psychologically is as difficult and delicate a task as is ever encountered in the mental health field.

Some professionals recommend that the problem be solved by switching the children's custody and home base by placing them in the home of the targeted parent.[4, 5] On the surface, this may appear to be a useful remedy for the targeted parent. But consideration must be given to what this sudden shift of home environment may do to the children. These are children who have been very thoroughly convinced that the targeted parent is their enemy—someone who is not to be relied upon for protection, who is unsafe to be with, and who does not love them. Sending them to live in such a home may be akin to ordering them into enemy territory. Simultaneously, these children fear losing the love and loyalty of the parent to whom they are most attached and upon whom they are most dependent.

Our experience of children who have had their residences switched in this manner is that the switch does not in many instances provide a happy outcome or a quick and uncomplicated remedy. Other clinicians and researchers are reaching similar conclusions.[6] These children are often genuinely frightened of the targeted parent; instead of easily learning to reexperience that parent as safe and loving, they are terrified and rejecting. They may become constricted, anxious, and unhappy children who maintain their psychological allegiance to the alienating parent—with whom they have the stronger bond. Even though the attachment may be an unhealthy one, it is the only one. They therefore long to be reunited with him or her. If they are young, they are unlikely to be emotionally equipped to sort out the reality of their parents' conflict and animosity; nor are they likely to recognize that they have been programmed or persuaded. As they grow older, the programming has often been integrated into their personalities. They sincerely believe that they want to be with and are happiest with the alienating parent, and they are afraid and frightened living with the targeted parent. Rather than thriving, unfolding, and blossoming—as the court and mental health professions who institute this change hope they will—these children often become shut down and emotionally constricted. Their sense of safety and emotional well-being may well have been compromised.

The problem of parental alienation is complex, far-reaching, and long-standing. There is no quick and easy solution for it. Recognizing it as early as possible is critical to preventing its long-term impact on children's personality development. When parental alienation escapes recognition until it reaches serious proportions, much more complex and time-consuming therapeutic and remediation efforts must be put in place to keep it from going any further. Sometimes, unfortunately, it cannot be stopped at all. Occasionally, the alienation has progressed to a point where nothing the legal or mental health system does will turn it around; the child is so completely alienated from one parent that no visitation or contact is possible. The child steadfastly and vehemently refuses to see or have contact with the other parent.

When this happens, time is the last resort. Most children eventually become curious about a rejected parent—usually during adolescence or early adulthood. Many of these children will suffer an especially tempestuous adolescent rebellion when they realize that the custodial parent has manipulated them and fostered their dependence.[7] Having developed sufficient autonomy to loosen their dependence on the alienating parent, they may seek out the absent parent to judge for themselves. Parents who have been estranged from their children by parental alienation should, therefore, find a way to maintain contact, letting their children know how to reach them when and if they want to reestablish old ties on a new basis.

This sad loss of the intervening years can be averted only by early recognition of the parental alienation syndrome by mental health and legal professionals familiar with its distinguishing features. At present, however, few training programs in the legal or mental health professions provide coursework in the underlying dynamics of the syndrome, the tactics employed by alienating parents, or the methods used to counteract the syndrome. Most professionals first become aware of parental alienation when a targeted parent realizes that he or she is being pushed out of a child's life and raises the alarm. By then, much of the damage may already have been done.

How Does Parental Alienation Develop?

Before attempting to prevent or treat the effects of the parental
alienation syndrome in any particular case, it is important to
understand how it comes about. To do so, it is necessary to
consider the predisposing family and individual dynamics and
their interaction with the situational factors that foster its development at the time of or following the divorce.

Family Dynamics

Often the groundwork for parental alienation is laid during the
years of the marriage or even earlier, in one parent's family of
origin. Parents at high risk of becoming involved in an alienating relationship often display a distinctive style of family life
prior to the divorce. They are likely to create an unusually
closed family system marked by limited interaction with the
outside world and mistrust of outsiders. Family members are
often involved with each other to the exclusion of other relationships. The children may be home-schooled or educated in a
closely controlled social or religious organization. Sometimes
one parent is still financially or emotionally dependent on his
or her own parents. He or she may telephone them frequently,
seek their advice about major decisions, and allow them to set
the tone and flavor of family life.

An allied characteristic of potentially alienating parents is
the family's reliance on "externalizing defenses" to manage
conflict. Failing to recognize their own part in creating a problem, they blame it on someone outside the family. Everything
becomes the fault of some outsider. While overuse of alcohol
and other abuses may contribute to the unhappiness of these
families, their most conspicuous characteristic is their closed
way of life.

During their marriage, these couples characteristically do
not develop effective ways to resolve personal conflicts between
themselves. The tendency to blame others reinforces their lack
of insight into their own behavior, and vice versa. As long as
the family is intact, outsiders can be blamed for all difficulties.

Once the couple is separated, however, the alienating parent tends to blame the other for more and more and to display little or no sadness about the breakup of the marriage.

Individual Dynamics

People with a self-protective personality style are at risk of becoming alienating parents. This style, which emerges early in life, results from being denied the right to express feelings of pain, shame, and anger. It may arise from experiences of abuse or neglect, from lack of respect for one's personal boundaries, or from a parent's unhealthy identification with an alienating parent as a child. Little by little, as these children learned to deny their feelings, their awareness of them was blunted. Buffered from their own pain, they eventually ceased to recognize or acknowledge it.

Very often the denial becomes a fixed, and effective, style of coping with the outside world. As adults these people function well in superficial relationships. They may be enormously successful in their careers, perhaps owning or managing a company with great success. They may even handle the logistics of caring for a family with competence and creativity. Often the self-protective personality style formed early in life works well on the outside.

One the inside, however, one basic function is missing. These people lack the capacity for intimacy, that is, the ability to understand and experience the feelings of others, to recognize the impact of their own behavior on others, and to allow to others the feelings and experiences evoked by their mutual interaction. After years of denying their own pain, they cannot feel the pain of others. This missing capacity is frequently reflected in a lack of empathy for their own children. They are not consciously or maliciously cold or uncaring people; they are simply who and what they have become.

They have little anxiety or self-insight. Individuals encased in self-protective outer layers are comfortable with who they are and see others as the problem. While inflexibly opposed to altering their own behavior, they are quick to assert that those around them need to change. They minimally acknowledge the loss and pain associated with divorce, for such feelings have been buried since childhood. Instead, they blame the other parent, sometimes becoming zealous in their need to label him or her as "bad" or to be publicly declared the "good" parent in a court or custody proceeding.

Individuals with this personality style are prime candidates for parental alienation. Being quickly aroused to anger, they react to criticisms of their parenting with intense rage and bear long-lasting grudges against those they believe have demeaned or harmed them. To them the world is a constantly threatening place, and they may find hidden evidence of this threat in ordinary or random events. They may exploit others, even their children, for their own purposes. They often do not distinguish between their own needs and those of their children.

Other patterns of individual dynamics present similar indicators of parental alienation. Individuals with a strong sense of entitlement have a need to see themselves as the best, the most glamorous, the most desirable or well-loved person. They often interpret divorce as betrayal and feel it as an enormous insult to their sense of self. For others, whose personalities manifest suspicious or paranoid features, the divorce confirms a basic belief system acquired early in life: only by maintaining careful guard at all times can they prevent other people from taking advantage of, humiliating, and demeaning them. Sadly, individuals with these personality styles experience great difficulty in expressing the pain and sadness of the divorce. They respond, instead, by blaming and devaluing their ex-spouse, sincerely believing that the children will be better having limited or no contact with him or her.

Situational Factors

Frequently the circumstances surrounding the divorce and separation trigger the alienation syndrome among people with these personality patterns. Although an alienating parent may use the particular situation principally as a smokescreen, a way to focus blame and avoid self-reflection, it is helpful to recognize the factors that commonly set the syndrome in motion. In fact, identifying these factors may well be the key to controlling the onset, intensity, and duration of the parental alienation syndrome, especially when understood in conjunction with predisposing individual and family dynamics.

For an individual unable to experience or tolerate his or her own pain, the most powerful situational factors are those that threaten to breach the protective outer layer built up over so many years. Instead of responding to the loss of the spouse and intact family with grief and distress, these parents are prone to become enormously angry. Almost immediately their anger may escalate into a sense of entitlement; the ex-spouse may be reviled and ultimately denounced as unworthy of a relationship with the children. Four situational factors very commonly incite this reaction.

Infidelity. In infidelity the pain of rejection by a loved one is accompanied by a powerful message that another person is preferred and desired. For most people this is deeply painful. Even within a marital relationship that remains intact, such a crisis can take years to work through. For parents with the family style and underlying personality structure described above, infidelity is profoundly shattering. It triggers feelings of personal humiliation and betrayal and demolishes the strongly enmeshed family unit. It can set in motion an alienation syndrome in which the unfaithful partner is labeled immoral and an unfit parent.

Remarriage. Occasionally a couple who have been divorced for some time and have successfully managed their children's visits suddenly burst into conflict over visitation. Often the unexpected breakdown is caused by the remarriage of the noncustodial parent. The dynamics are similar to those described for infidelity, inasmuch as remarriage also represents confirmation that another person is the preferred love object. Certain individuals experience an ex-spouse's remarriage as a definitive, and public, repudiation of themselves.

Remarriage also means that there will now be a stepparent in the ex-spouse's home. His or her presence during visits may represent a threat to the bond between the children and their biological parent. If the new stepparent pushes for increased visitation or moves too quickly into a nurturing role, the threatened parent may begin to show signs of becoming an alienating parent.

Postdivorce Sadness. Typically, even parents who desired the divorce experience ambivalence, second thoughts, and sadness over what might have been. Mourning the broken family unit, redefining oneself as acceptable and lovable, and restructuring the family into two homes and a visiting arrangement are all part of the painful process of divorce. Some individuals, however, find the accompanying pain too overwhelming to enable themselves to recover a confident self-concept.

Like the self-protective individuals described in the preceding section, they may have missed the nurturance they needed as young children and learned to protect themselves by refusing to acknowledge pain. Lacking a capacity for self-insight, they are unprepared for the emotional ramifications of the divorce decision. They may have sought the divorce out of a desire for revenge or to teach the partner a lesson. They may even believe that the threat of divorce will cause the spouse to return to the marriage with an enhanced view of themselves. When this scenario fails to be realized and the marriage breaks down, such parents vehemently and angrily reject the departing spouse. Underneath the anger there is enormous sadness and pain, and occasionally some of it breaks through. More often, the veneer remains intact.

As a result of their early deprivation, these parents are not likely to have learned to soothe and comfort themselves. They may therefore seek solace in their children. The bond between parent and children becomes more and more intense as the latter take over the role of comforters. In these circumstances, to share the children with an ex-spouse is to risk losing them and the means of maintaining self-esteem and warding off depression. The situation is ripe for the development of an alienation syndrome.

Sudden Marital Breakdown. A small percentage of marriages end quickly and dramatically. One partner abruptly enters into a new romantic relationship, abandoning the family with no explanation. Or a battered spouse or one who can no longer bear the regimen of an extremely controlling partner may abandon him or her.

Regardless of the reason, sudden marital breakdown short-circuits a number of important psychological processes. The abandoned partner is left to reconstruct an understanding of why the marriage failed on his or her own. Being left without warning provides no opportunity to prepare oneself physically, financially, and emotionally. Resentment of and anger at the departing spouse are normal responses. It is easy to label the parent who leaves the "bad guy." Even an empathic parent may find it difficult to encourage a relationship between the children and such an "unworthy" individual. Parents who have trouble maintaining self-esteem and accepting rejection because of their own personality dynamics will be even more likely to focus the blame unrelentingly on the other parent and to display the characteristic features of parents who alienate.

Because situational factors like these may precipitate the cycle of alienation, they are highly useful early indicators of future trouble. Legal and mental health professionals need to be especially attuned to situations—whether infidelity, remarriage, sudden abandonment, or some other situation—that a parent with such predisposing individual dynamics will interpret as betrayal.

The Tools of Alienation

In addition to understanding these interpersonal and individual dynamics and situational factors, professionals alert to early signs of parental alienation will learn to recognize the tactics alienating parents use. As we suggested earlier in this chapter, most divorced parents harbor some degree of animosity for each other and will occasionally employ some of these tactics. The preponderant and unrelenting use of the techniques discussed below is the key to differentiating between essentially healthy parents and those at risk for the alienation syndrome.

Denial and Devaluation

The alienating parent denies the importance and value of the other parent at all levels. His or her very existence may be denied by removing photographs and destroying all evidence that the other parent ever lived in the home or was married to the alienating parent. The other parent is never referred to or acknowledged in front of the children. If he or she shows up at a school or recreational activity, the alienating parent avoids all contact, even eye contact. The unspoken message to the child is: "Do not look over there. Do not even act as if you have seen your mother or father. His or her presence is of no importance." When the child returns from a visit to the other parent, the alienating parent shows no interest in what has happened there. If the child is assertive enough to express pleasure in some activity he or she enjoyed, the alienating parent is quick to discount it as trivial and unimportant. Having a good time visiting with the other parent is tantamount to an act of disloyalty. Children quickly get the message and comply.[9]

Telephone messages, mail, gifts, and other forms of communication from the victimized parent may be destroyed or ignored. If they are passed on to the children, it is with disdain: "Doesn't your father know you are much too old for that toy? We'll give it to your little cousin." Or "Mom knows we don't celebrate Christmas, and Hanukkah was over two weeks ago. I'll drive you to the mall, and you can put these in the box for needy children who don't get many Christmas toys."

Even the legitimate rescheduling of a visit may be used to sabotage a targeted parent. One mother who was informed that her son's weekly visit with his father would have to be canceled because of the latter's illness allowed the six-year-old to pack his bag as usual and sit by the window waiting to be picked up. When his father failed to appear, she held up his absence as evidence he was unreliable and uncaring.[8]

Exaggerating Unfavorable Traits

We all have personality traits or aspects of our day-to-day behavior that could be improved. The alienating parent is an expert at pointing out these faults and exaggerating them into major defects. The mother who is often late is an easy target, giving the father a chance to imply that she doesn't care enough to be on time or to call the child as promised. The father whose housekeeping is a little casual or who is a bit lax about unimportant details of caretaking may be labeled a "slob who can't even do the most menial job correctly." As soon as children return from a visit, the alienating parent may carefully inspect them, pronounce them dirty or unkempt, and send them off to shower and change.

Tribal Warfare

Tribal warfare is a term employed by researchers to describe a tactic common in high-conflict divorce.[9] One parent extends the conflict well beyond the immediate family arena by telling neighbors, friends, and colleagues confidential details about disputes. Others may be encouraged, intentionally or inadvertently, to take sides and to express contempt for the targeted parent, often in front of the children. The children are soon likely to be surrounded by a large network of people who seem to share the belief that their other parent is despicable. In addition, the ex-spouse's family, parents, and friends often come under attack; even his or her work associates and neighbors may be openly maligned.

Putting Children in the Middle

We have mentioned before that alienating parents frequently discuss with their children issues that should be worked out between adults. Very frequently, financial concerns are at the center of these discussions. One day Ilana, a twelve-year-old girl, walked into her father's bedroom and found him openly crying as he wrote out the checks for his monthly bills. When she expressed her sympathy, her father told her what a hard time he was having financially. He claimed that the girl's mother, on the other hand, had a rich boyfriend who bought her lavish gifts and ensured that she would have no money worries. He also distorted the facts, claiming that he was obligated to pay her child support if he wanted to continue seeing Ilana.

It is also very common for parents to thrust children into adult discussions not only about finances but also about visitation and scheduling. An alienating parent may encourage them to say they don't like to visit or that they want to go less often or not at all. Concerns about a targeted parent's dubious judgment or moral character may be used as an excuse to push children into interparental conflicts: "Please inform your mother that the movie you saw last weekend upset you so much you couldn't get to sleep" or "Tell your dad to see his bimbos on his own time."

Inciting Emotional Outbursts

Probably no one is more acutely aware of a person's emotional vulnerabilities than an ex-spouse. Consciously or unconsciously, an alienating parent may incite a targeted parent to anger, tears or confused distress in front of the child, effectively demonstrating the weakness of the other's character. Goading a parent into a frightening display of anger at transition times sends the child an especially potent message: "How scary to go off with someone so out of control! You would be much safer here with me."

All these tactics of parental alienation can be used in degrees ranging from unspoken yet insidious undermining of the parent–child relationship to volatile and openly hostile attacks. By learning to identify them early, legal and mental health professionals may be able to identify the parental alienation syndrome in time to take effective action to stop this destructive polarization.

Too often, however, both attorneys and mental health professionals are themselves drawn into the alienation process and end up polarized as well. An attorney, or a therapist to one parent, generally hears only the side of his or her own client and may not even meet the other parent. From their vantage points, neither professional may be able to sort out false from truthful allegations of harm or even potential abuse. A mental health professional treating the children may be subject to the same pressures as the children; that is, the expectation of validating the notion of the "harmfulness" of one parent.

Cases of parental alienation syndrome sometimes come to light when the children or one of the parents is referred for assessment or treatment. However, both individual therapy for the alienating parent alone and family therapy alone are relatively ineffective ways to treat the complex interplay of the internal and situational dynamics that cause the syndrome. What is needed is a comprehensive treatment approach that addresses all the contributing factors and is carried out by a team of professionals trained in family law, conflict resolution and mediation, and child development. We present such a comprehensive intervention model in the next chapter.

7

A Comprehensive Intervention Model for Parental Alienation

The remediation model we present in this chapter takes into account the complex nature of parental alienation and suggests a balanced and multifaceted intervention approach. If it is to be successful, attorneys and mental health professionals on both sides will need to work together. There must be a minimization of the win-or-lose strategy. First and foremost, therefore, we emphasize that for families and children caught in the stresses of parental alienation, litigation is likely to exacerbate the polarization.

By its very nature, litigation determines blame and punishes guilty parties. A strategy of alienating parents, similarly, is to convince an authority to pronounce them worthy and their ex-spouses bad parents. Court proceedings often undermine healing and reinforce alienating parents' principal emotional defenses: denial of painful feelings and the tendency to blame others for their problems. If they lose the court battle, alienating parents are even less likely to build insight and to heal; they will probably be outraged by the public humiliation and the failure of the system to acknowledge their point of view. In such cases the conflict is likely to escalate, and the children are likely to remain in the middle of their parents' battles. A coordinated effort to implement a comprehensive model of intervention is the children's best hope of a better outcome.

The intervention model we recommend consists of four distinct and simultaneous intervention components:

- the parenting coordinator
- the children's therapy
- strategies for the targeted parent
- strategies for the alienated parent

The Parenting Coordinator

If alienation is suspected, the court could appoint a parenting coordinator to implement a shared-parenting plan. This pivotal person may be a mental health professional, a court-appointed guardian, or a well-trained paraprofessional. It is essential that he or she be familiar with family law, conflict resolution, and mediation as well as family therapy and child development.

As the first-line decision maker, the coordinator's position and powers must be specified in a binding legal agreement among all the parties. (See Appendix C for a sample Parenting Coordinator Agreement.) Depending on the circumstances, he or she may report regularly to the court or a court-appointed guardian or, alternatively, may decide to keep all communications confidential. Neither parent can fire the coordinator for a prespecified period of time, perhaps (as a guideline) one to two years. If at the end of the specified time a decision is made to end the relationship with the particular professional, the court may appoint a new coordinator if it determines that the parents remain enmeshed in conflict. If the alienating parent moves out of the state with the children, the court should order that a new parenting coordinator be appointed where the children now reside.

The parenting coordinator may be ultimately responsible for all decisions regarding implementation of the visitation schedule and any modifications made in it, or he or she may elect to delegate the arbitrator role to another professional. He or she hears all points of view, is available to mediate solutions, and disseminates relevant information about decisions to the appropriate parties. Because of the coordinator's critical role in maintaining communications, the court must ensure that he or she will have access to both parents, their attorneys (if desired by the coordinator), the children's therapists, and all other professionals, teachers, and caretakers involved with the children.

The parenting coordinator bears a tremendous responsibility for making shared parenting work in alienated families. He or she must, therefore, be well trained in child development and knowledgeable about what constitutes appropriate visitation for children of different ages. Because children in alienating families frequently refuse to comply fully with the visitation schedule, or even to visit one parent at all, the coordinator may well become the sole link between the targeted parent and the children. Whether the noncustodial parent lives in another state or in the same town, he or she may need to send mail and gifts for the children through the coordinator. The coordinator may arrange to have the children visit the office once a week or as necessary to pick up mail and telephone the targeted parent.

The parenting coordinator decides when the children are ready to resume or increase visits to the targeted parent. As children of high-conflict divorce may not be ready for visitation schedules designed for other children their age, initial visits may be brief and may take place in a supervised setting. These children will probably move slowly toward longer, unsupervised visits; in fact, it may take as much as a year or even several years to achieve that goal. In the meantime, the parent–child relationship can be augmented by letters and telephone calls. As they mature and become increasingly independent, most children will be able to make longer and less structured visits.

Whatever the visits' duration and form, alienating parents will probably oppose them vehemently. Under the agreement, these parents will address their grievances to the parenting coordinator. Parents whose conscious or unconscious goal is to impede the relationship between their children and the targeted parent may present very convincing arguments against allowing visits. They may even threaten to file a grievance against the parenting coordinator. The latter must, therefore, be a person of professional firmness and tact, able to withstand threats or allegations of the dangers presented by visitation. Sticking to the established plan, the coordinator must form his or her own judgment about the children's safety and, if in doubt, call in an expert to assess the situation.

The most effective coordinator will possess not only an aura of authority but also a high degree of skill in dispute resolution. A court ruling giving him or her the power to arbitrate disputes or delegating arbitration power to another professional will be helpful. The parenting coordinator, more than likely, will bear the brunt of some of the parents' anger, freeing the children's therapists to concentrate on building effective therapeutic alliances with the children.

Without a coordinator, the therapists would be forced to take sides in making decisions about visitation. They would thus be subject to the persuasive tactics of alienating parents and, ultimately, to threats to terminate therapy for not complying with their wishes. In such an adversarial atmosphere, therapeutic relationships would be compromised. Moreover, a therapist simultaneously mediating between highly conflicted parents is less likely to fulfill the therapeutic goal of focusing solely on the child's needs. At some point, the therapist is likely to offend a parent, perhaps provoking the parent to want to find a new therapist, and the child will lose an important ally and have to reestablish trust in a new therapeutic relationship. Each time it is repeated, this process of reengagement in therapy becomes increasingly difficult and hopes for successful treatment decline.

Protecting the neutrality of the children's therapy is thus a critical component of interventions in cases of alienation syndrome.

The Children's Therapy

Children of divorce caught in an alienating situation are at high risk for later pathology caused by compromises to their sense of individuality. The subtle message of an alienating parent— usually the custodial parent—is clear to children: "You must

see things my way or you won't be loved and cared for," or
"you are betraying me and my needs." The high price paid for
that love is habitual denial of the sense of self.

Lacking the freedom to form their own opinions or to express a desire to spend time with the targeted parent, children
grow to doubt their own feelings. They rely increasingly on
others to make judgments for them. When encouraged to see
the divorce through the eyes of the alienating parent, as they
frequently are, these children are forced to repress normal
feelings of loss and grief that are a part of the divorce process.
They fail to receive the compassionate understanding of their
feelings of loss that children need during the first few years of
a divorce. Instead, they are placed squarely in the middle of
the conflict and are encouraged to take sides, to express others' feelings, and to reject one of their parents. Permission to
love and maintain a relationship with both parents—one of
the essential healing factors for children of divorce—is sadly
lacking.

Most children will experience stress when they are forced to
deny their feelings in this way. They may express it in peer or
social problems, school adjustment issues, somatic symptoms,
or irrational temper tantrums. Alienating parents frequently
interpret such signs of stress as confirmation that the children
would be better off if the targeted parent's visits were further
limited or were totally absent from their lives.

The risk is lifelong. Giving up their sense of self and individuality and learning ways to deny instead of express the normal
pains of life set them on the same sad road that the alienating
parent has traveled. They, too, learn to buffer themselves
against authentic feeling and risk the same chance of developing a crippled capacity for intimacy.

For these children, there is significant benefit if there is one
person who can provide a sense of validation for their feelings—a person to whom they can express the pain of the conflict, the fears and anxieties that come from being caught in the
middle, and the frustration of being prohibited from loving or
expressing the love for one of their parents. Neither parent can
serve as such an individual without deepening the children's

loyalty bind; nor can relatives and friends drawn into the conflict on one side or the other fill such a role.

A neutral person is therefore critical. The children's therapist can provide a sheltered setting, a place where children have the freedom to share their pain, form their own opinions, and develop a sense of self separate from the alienating parent. If the therapist becomes yet another participant in the divorce dispute, however, the benefits children can gain from therapy may be severely diminished.

Before therapy can begin, therefore, both parents and their attorneys must sign an agreement stipulating that the children's therapist will not be involved in any legal proceedings. (Appendix D provides a sample Child Therapist Agreement.) For the same reason, the therapist will share with the parenting coordinator—but not with either parent—reports on the progress of therapy and on aspects of the child's dynamics that are important for parents to understand and use to guide their decision making. Any information related to legal matters will also be channeled to the appropriate parties through the parenting coordinator.

Both parents should be consulted about the initial selection of the therapist. Once he or she is appointed, however, ongoing contact between therapist and parents should be limited. It is likely that at these times the alienating parent will attempt to communicate damaging views of the targeted parent. The skilled therapist will be adept at setting conversational boundaries and avoiding involvement in interparental disputes. He or she will thus demonstrate to the children that the therapeutic process provides a degree of protection from conflict.

The therapist to children victimized by alienation tactics needs to be especially well versed in divorce-related issues from a developmental perspective and capable of maintaining neutrality. He or she will, of course, be aware that the alienating parent may be putting words in the children's mouths on the way to therapy and encouraging them to give the therapist only information that is negative regarding the targeted parent. On the drive home as well, the parent may press the child to divulge what went on during therapy.

For this and other reasons, the pace and progress of therapy will be slow. Most children in alienating families are highly mistrustful, slow to warm up, and wary of sharing their thoughts and feelings. The therapist will need ample time to earn their trust and carry out the goals of therapy. If the child–therapist relationship is not protected from interference, alienating parents are likely to terminate therapy if they feel that the therapist will not join the alliance against the targeted parent. Consequently, although alienating parents should have some input into the initial selection of a therapist, only the parenting coordinator and the therapist should determine when the children's therapy has achieved its goals and can be terminated.

During the initial meeting with the child, the therapist will describe and support the legal and procedural boundaries to which all parties have agreed. Throughout therapy, the therapist will assure the child that the therapy hour is for the child alone and that the therapy room is a safe place in which to express feelings. Together, the therapist and the child or children will explore issues critical to the goal of identifying their own emotions and using them to shape judgments and decisions.

In this context, the therapist will listen carefully for *dissonance,* that is, contradictions that grow out of children's experiences with both parents. Dissonance occurs when a child experiences the targeted parent as different from the image created by the alienating parent. By focusing on the identification of independence in thinking and in judgment—first in terms of experiences outside the family and gradually focusing on the family—the therapist can gradually help children begin to construct an independent view of a parent. For example, a child might describe how Dad helped select and pay for a birthday present for the child's friend. He or she might then wonder why Mom said Dad was stingy. The image the child has carried of Dad as penny-pinching has been challenged, however slightly, by the difference between this experience and Mom's assertion. The therapist should listen carefully for the emergence of such dissonance and point it out to the child when it occurs.

Once children become conscious of a disparity between their own experience of the targeted parent and the alienating parent's characterizations, they will need help handling some difficult moments. The therapist will empathize with how hard it is to manage the alienating parent's intrusive questioning. At these times, children especially appreciate learning simple answers they can use to protect their personal boundaries.

Children of alienating parents are also likely to need help integrating the experience of the divorce itself. Being egocentric by nature, children frequently assume that all children of divorce face very similar experiences. In reality, only a small percentage of children of divorce are caught up in high conflict and, specifically, in alienating situations. Hearing what divorce is like for other children can encourage them to look to the future with more hope.

The most important goal of the children's therapy, therefore, is the emergence of a separate sense of self. The therapist will see that self emerging when children begin to internalize images of their parents based on their own experiences rather than on the viewpoints of others.

The older the child, the easier this process will be. Children under six have great difficulty with ambivalence; they barely understand that a person can have two different or contradictory feelings at the same time. Younger children are also very dependent on the parent's direct reassurances of love. Children between six and twelve will vary in their tolerance of ambivalent or contradictory feelings. They are likely to require more time in therapy to accomplish the goal of claiming their own thoughts, feelings, and opinions. Children over twelve sometimes undertake this kind of self-examination on their own as a more confident sense of self emerges during adolescence. Nonetheless, they, too, will need support and guidance. Sometimes the rejection of one parent remains steadfast throughout adolescence and the development of an independent sense of self does not emerge until early adulthood.

Strategies for the Targeted Parent

Targeted parents either have already been pushed out of their children's lives or are at imminent risk of rejection. Their children may be refusing visitation altogether, visiting them infrequently, or coming only as sullen messengers of the alienating parent's criticisms and complaints.

When children become bearers of messages that obviously reflect the feelings of the alienating parent, targeted parents are apt to respond defensively. Often the child gives away the source of the message by using adult-sounding phrases or bringing up adult issues. One nine-year-old- girl, for example, asked her father when he was going to start sending the amount of child support specified in the court decree. If the targeted father had yielded to the temptation to argue her into a different view of the situation, he would have enmeshed her more deeply in a loyalty bind. Dependent as she was on the alienating mother, the child was unlikely to switch her allegiance.

Targeted parents are frequently angry parents. They are mad at the system, which they believe has permitted the other parent to separate them from their children. They feel wronged. They want change and look to legal and mental health professionals for more efficient justice and acknowledgment of their worth. Often they are in a hurry to resume visitation on a schedule suitable to their children's ages. Unfortunately, undoing alienation is not so simple. It may be a lengthy process that calls for extraordinary patience. If they hurry to regain parental "rights," targeted parents may only make things worse. Targeted parents need to understand that a court order cannot mandate a healthy, supportive parent/child relationship; nor does number of hours or overnights assure a positive parent/child relationship. The targeted parent can only attain this by building and strengthening the relationship with the child directly.

Many targeted parents, therefore, can benefit enormously from psychotherapy that helps them identify ways of rebuilding a relationship with their children. A specific focus on gradually building empathy and connectedness with their children is critical and may be the first step toward remedying alienation. This is especially true for targeted parents who were not closely involved in their children's lives before the divorce. A relationship of trust between children and a parent who was underinvolved in meeting their needs in the past may be fragile and easily eroded by interparental conflict. An alienating parent who bore most of the responsibility for childrearing during the marriage is likely to monopolize even more of the parenting functions after the divorce. One of the important jobs of targeted parents, therefore, is mastering the logistics of single parenting, learning how to meet their children's unique needs while gaining enjoyment and satisfaction from doing so.

Learning techniques and gaining support for managing anger is another crucial task of therapy for the targeted parent. There are a number of ways to learn to contain rage and to respond dispassionately to the myriad provocations of alienation. Improving communication skills, developing conscious awareness of the triggers for anger, and building self-esteem can all help. The therapeutic process needs to focus on feeling in control by anticipating, not controlling or preventing, the undermining behaviors of the alienating parent. Maturity and detachment can be built as targeted parents learn to identify and speak of their own assets as parents. One goal of therapy for these parents is to help them hear criticism of their own behavior without reacting with defensive anger. Responding with anger can only reinforce their children's low opinion of them.

Often children have a genuine fear of the targeted parent's anger, a fear alienating parents are quick to reinforce by emphasizing the threat inherent in its explosiveness. Even if targeted parents currently have every reason to be angry, they need to accept responsibility for inappropriate displays of anger in the past. They should explain to the children how they are attempting to change their ways of coping with and resolving conflict. Only when targeted parents learn to contain and control their anger do children have the opportunity to experience the dissonance described earlier which allows for independent thinking and relationship building. Justifying inappropriate behavior by blaming others will not solve the alienation problem. Staying calm, working toward constructive conflict resolution, and learning not to take the highly charged emotional bait that is offered are enormous emotional tasks, but they are not impossible to achieve. Frequently mastery of these techniques and approaches helps ease the pain and build self-esteem.

Another area in which targeted parents usually need guidance is in taking the children out of the middle of the conflict. This can be done by explaining to the children that there are two sides to most problems. False allegations can be reframed in a very brief, preferably two-or-three-sentence, explanation. For example, if a child says to the targeted parent, "Mom says you're a liar. You didn't pay her what you agreed to in court," the father might respond with, "I feel I paid what I promised. The court has guidelines for this, and they will help your mother and me work this out. This is not something you need to worry about." Many times the most reassuring explanation parents can offer is that adults will deal with the issue and that children will be spared the burden of another loyalty bind. Children need frequent messages of love and caring from both parents far more than they need explanations of adult issues.

Earlier we mentioned that alienating parents often point to a targeted parent's weaknesses, exaggerating them into evidence of serious character defects. We used an example of a mother whose repeated lateness picking up the children for the weekend gave the alienating father an opportunity to cast doubt on her feelings for them: "She doesn't care enough about you to get here on time." Instead of responding angrily to such an allegation, which contained some truth and a good deal of exaggeration, the targeted parent could accept ownership of some parts of it, perhaps reframing the situation in a different perspective. She might, for example, respond by saying, "It's true that I have trouble being on time, and I'm sorry if it causes you to worry. But I love having you with me, and I always make sure to get here for our visits."

Being a targeted parent is often unfair. Targeted parents need to know that they are not alone. A support group led by a trained professional and composed of people in similar circumstances may be a beneficial adjunct to individual pscyhotherapy. Besides mutual understanding, group members can often teach each other techniques for maintaining positive parenting relationships despite periods of high stress. A group may also provide a safe place to practice accepting criticism and learning to reframe it in a constructive way.

In individual therapy and in groups, targeted parents need a good deal of support to accept the reality of the situation, to remain patient, and to develop the skills necessary to change. They should not expect immediate relief from the legal or mental health system. Ultimately, targeted parents themselves hold the power to loosen the loyalty bind their children are caught in. Allowing their children to experience them as loving, caring, accessible, competent, and nurturing is the best route to healing. With time and effort, they may be able to rebuild a healthy relationship with their children.

Strategies for the Alienating Parent

Although it might appear that the parental alienation syndrome stems from the behavior of one parent, the situation is rarely this simple. As noted earlier, alienation is the result of a complex interplay of interpersonal dynamics and situational factors. To be successful, a treatment plan must be comprehensive enough to address all of them. In our experience, the most frequently recommended remedy for alienation, ordering the alienating parent into therapy as the only treatment component, has been only minimally helpful.

Alienating parents tend to experience little benefit from therapy. Often lacking the capacity for self-insight, they are generally unable to acknowledge their own personal distress or to see that they have contributed to the problem. To themselves, and often to others, they appear to be in control, so their motivation for change is minimal.

Alienating parents also have a remarkable talent for compounding the conflict by drawing others into it. If they are ordered into therapy, they will often shop around until they find a therapist who supports their view of the situation. Moreover, in empathizing with a client, many therapists are unwittingly drawn into seeing the situation entirely from the client's point of view. With clients like these, even the most skilled therapist may have difficulty setting limits and avoiding manipulation.

Achieving change in a person's fundamental personality may take years of therapy. Alienating parents are unlikely to last the course; they tend to drop out if they are not fully supported or are challenged in some way. Even when they remain in therapy, they may not make good use of it. In the meantime, the relationship between the targeted parent and the children suffers enormous damage.

For this reason, individual therapy for the alienating parent can be only one component of an overall treatment plan. If it is utilized, the therapist should be a member of a comprehensive intervention plan headed by the parenting coordinator.

Children Who Refuse Visitation

One of the hallmarks of the alienation syndrome is the child who refuses age-appropriate visitation. When this occurs, the parenting coordinator must first gain a thorough understanding of the issues interfering with successful visitation. A careful assessment of the situation from the perspective of each child in the family can be made directly, by interviewing them, or indirectly, by discussions with the children's therapists.

Individual assessment of the children will enable the parenting coordinator to tailor a visitation schedule to the age and particular needs of each child. A four-year-old boy, for example, may have different feelings about visiting than his ten-year-old sister. At the same time, he may be reassured by her presence during visits, a fact the coordinator will take into consideration in designing a visitation plan for the family.

The purpose of visitation is to build or maintain a relationship between the children and the nonresidential parent. If the child is frightened during the visits, no relationship can be built. Thus, one of the first tasks in designing visitation is to determine what each child needs to feel safe and relatively comfortable. Eliminating all anxiety may be impossible, as

alienating parents will probably continue efforts to consciously or unconsciously convince the children that visiting
the other parent is disloyal or dangerous. When this happens,
the goal must be to keep anxiety to a manageable level for
each child.

Some children are more resilient than others, or simply more
mature and able to reach outside the family for reassurance.
Others display considerable anxiety when first separated from
the alienating parent but, after the difficult transition, are able
to enjoy the visit without distress. In determining the level of
anxiety that is manageable for each child in a family, the coordinator will need to consider not only their ages but also
their different temperaments and the ascribed role they play in
the family. When the needs of children in the family vary
greatly, either each child will have an individualized visitation
plan or all the children will start at the visitation level of the
most vulnerable child.

Refusal to visit can also be manifested with different degrees
of intensity and determination. Some children caught in an
alienation situation remain willing to visit according to a carefully prescribed schedule that allows little or no leeway for
change. Because, as discussed earlier, most interparental conflict breaks out at transition times, it is often a good idea to
drop off and pick up children at a neutral location—at school
or a public location, such as a library, restaurant or shopping
mall if the city has no visitation services center.

Occasionally, children refusing age-appropriate visitation
will respond to the voice of authority. The parenting coordinator might explain that when parents divorce, the judge orders children to spend time with both their parents because it is
best for them. He or she may promise to work with the children
to make their visits successful and fun but may emphasize that
the judge has the clear authority to order the visits. Obviously,
the parenting coordinator will take this approach only after
determining that visits will not cause the children unmanage-
able levels of anxiety.

When children are clearly not ready for an age-appropriate

visitation schedule, the coordinator will plan a pared-down version suitable for a younger child. In all cases, the goal is to maintain as much visitation as the child can tolerate while moving in small steps toward a fuller schedule. For example, although most school-age children can handle a visit that includes at least one overnight stay, a child involved in alienation may be comfortable only with daytime visits. In this case, the parenting coordinator will have to back down from the recommended schedule for that age; he or she should retreat only as far as is necessary to contain the child's anxiety. For some children, this may mean major cutbacks in visiting time; for others, a small reduction may suffice.

Some children who have experienced high levels of parental conflict may be comfortable visiting the noncustodial parent only in the presence of another trusted adult. If so, the adult needs to be identified and his or her assistance sought. In a few cities there are now therapeutic visitation centers where a child and a parent can play or talk together in the presence of a therapist or another supervising adult.

Even this level of visitation may prove too much for young children caught in long-standing animosity and alienation. If a child must be practically pried loose knuckle by knuckle from the alienating parent in order to visit, visitation must simply be suspended until a greater level of comfort can be attained. In the interim every avenue to maintaining contact should be explored. Most children need to have indirect contact with the targeted parent through letters, telephone calls, small gifts, cards, or remembrances on a regular and predictable basis. As outlined in the section on the functions of the parenting coordinator, we recommend that children visit the office of the coordinator weekly to make telephone calls, open and read mail, and employ any other means of communication to maintain contact. For targeted parents, there are also a number of techniques for building a relationship from a distance that have been developed for parents who live far from their children.[1, 2] Whatever the method, the goal is to keep the relationship alive while, in therapy, the children evolve toward a separate sense of themselves and, ultimately, a reconceptualization of the targeted parent.

In serious cases of alienation this sort of progress may come very slowly. When children do show themselves ready for increased involvement and visitation, however, the parenting coordinator's decision must be firm. He or she should neither be influenced to move faster, because the targeted parent is frustrated and claims the "right" to increased visitation, nor be persuaded to stay at a minimal level of visitation by an alienating parent determined to restrict contact. When it is beneficial for the children, the parenting coordinator must independently steer a steady course toward increased contact and visitation.

When the parenting coordinator determines that children are ready for a more advanced level of visitation, he or she must have the power to effect it. The authority of the court and the parenting agreement must place full responsibility in the hands of the coordinator or arbitrator, limiting the possibility of litigation or further discussion. Although the children's therapist may be consulted by the coordinator, the therapeutic relationship needs protection from being compromised. If necessary, the therapist must clearly remind both parents of the agreement to insulate the children's therapy from parental disputes.

Some degree of conflict and animosity is likely to greet each recommendation for increased visitation. As children move toward a healthier relationship with the targeted parent, the alienating parent will feel threatened and will turn up the pressure of the tactics described in Chapter 6 as "tools of alienation." It cannot be stressed too strongly that the parenting coordinator must be a strong professional able to withstand relentless efforts at persuasion from both sides.

Just as important, he or she must be skilled at defusing conflict and offering parents ways to continue communicating. Such delicate undertakings assume a high level of knowledge and skill. The coordinator must first achieve a thorough understanding of the dynamics of the conflict at both the situational and the personal (intrapsychic) levels. He or she will then carefully plan responses that offer the kind of support and limits each parent needs. No single technique will work for all parents. The ability to tailor strategies to the underlying dynamics, to remain sensitive to the vulnerabilities of each parent, and so, to avoid triggering renewed conflict is critical. In Chapters 8 and 9, we discuss in detail techniques of conflict resolution sensitive to the dynamics between troubled parents.

Long-Distance Relationships

It is not uncommon for an alienating parent who has custody of the children to suddenly announce a move out of the state. Obviously such a change puts the relationship between the targeted parent and the children in even more jeopardy. Maintaining a long-distance parent–child relationship is difficult, even when parents cooperate well. For a family in conflict the risks of further alienation are far greater. We therefore recommend that the parenting coordinator assess the rationale for a long-distance move beforehand and report to the court on its likely impact on the children's relationship with the targeted parent. In some instances the court may intervene to prevent the move; in others it is powerless to do so.

If the move does take place, a new parenting coordinator must immediately be appointed in the new location. The children will also need a therapist in their new community. As he or she does when children are unable to handle direct contacts, the new coordinator will be responsible for helping the children maintain their relationship with the distant parent by mail and weekly telephone calls. The planning of visits—now a more complicated process—will continue to rest with the coordinator.

The new parenting coordinator should take the opportunity to meet with the targeted parent when he or she comes to visit the children. Ongoing telephone contact between the targeted parent and all professionals involved with the children will also help sustain the connection. Most important is the commitment of the parenting coordinator to support and maintain the relationship. Without it, children will be a high risk of losing a parent.

As we have outlined them in this chapter, the essential characteristics of an intervention in a case of parental alienation are a comprehensive approach, early identification, limitation of litigation, and the appointment of a parenting coordinator. Financially, the model may be costly. If it is necessary to economize, it is essential to retain the children's therapist and the parenting coordinator. They are the core of the intervention model.

8

Creating a Parenting Plan for High-Conflict Divorce

In most jurisdictions, a final divorce decree typically specifies physical custody arrangements, legal custody, and a visitation plan for the children. These elements may be negotiated by attorneys, formulated with the help of a mediator, or mandated by a judge. What cannot be mandated, however, is a couple's ability to carry out these arrangements in a way that minimizes their children's exposure to conflict.

In this chapter, we address this difficulty by presenting a model for conceptualizing the various levels of impasse reached by high-conflict divorcing couples. We then describe four personality types that are at high risk of reaching an impasse. Finally, we discuss the process of creating a parenting plan for couples whose unremitting conflict and inability to work together sabotage visitation arrangements. The discussion will be useful to legal and mental health professionals designing plans for couples who remain clenched in hostility long after the divorce. Parents who are themselves enmeshed in conflict will also gain insight into their own difficulties.

The first step in creating a workable parenting plan for such parents is identifying the individual characteristics, interpersonal dynamics, and situational factors that prevent successful implementation of the mandated visitation plan. Legal and mental health professionals working with a couple can then match their strategies to the particular family so as to insulate the children from interparental animosity.

For almost everyone, the initial stages of divorce are highly painful. Most people are angry and upset. Arguments occur frequently, and ex-spouses speak of each other with bitterness and scorn. Self-esteem has been battered by the pain of rejection and a sense of failure. Healing has not yet begun. Unfortunately, about 25 percent of divorced couples never get past this initial stage.[2] These are the couples who, three or more years later, still talk as if the divorce happened yesterday.

The Dynamics of Impasse

Mediators and researchers Janet Johnston and Linda Campbell, have studied the dynamics of the impasse reached by couples like these.[1] They suggest that the key to creating an effective parenting plan lies in working strategically, utilizing parents' existing defensive structures rather than attempting to remake entrenched, and usually lifelong, ego defenses. As we pointed out in our discussion of parental alienation, even long-term psychotherapy may not change a person's basic personality structure. Parents in conflict are often resistant to psychotherapy; they are likely to respond to criticism of their shortcomings or to direct confrontation by building defensive walls higher, thus undermining the goals of visitation. Nor do high-conflict couples necessarily respond well to traditional forms of mediation. They may lack the capacity to cooperate.

One couple like this was almost continuously in court. Frank and Marie disagreed vehemently about everything and seemed totally unable to prevent involving their children in the conflict. Exasperated, the judge ordered that they be given a workable co-parenting plan before they returned to court. Yet they had already gone through more than one excellent custody evaluation and been provided with several good visitation plans. The recommendations they had received sounded sensible, and they were reasonably intelligent people. Nonetheless, they had fought nonstop for the past three years at almost every drop-off and pickup. They even fought at their daughter's soccer games and school events.

Johnston and Campbell have proposed a model for conceptualizing the impasse reached by couples like these, who are still arguing two or more years after the divorce.[1] They describe these couples as locked at one or more of three levels of impasse (see Figure 8–1):

- the external-social level
- the interactional level
- the intrapsychic level

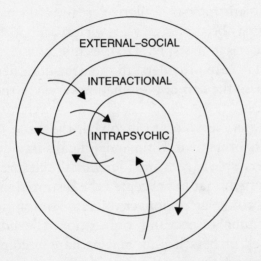

I. INTRAPSYCHIC LEVEL

Vulnerability to Loss

a. prior traumatic loss
b. separation-individuation conflicts: diffuse, counter- and oscillating dependency

Vulnerability to Humiliation/Shame

a. mild—specific acknowledgment
b. moderate—projects total blame
c. severe–paranoia

II. INTERACTIONAL LEVEL

a. legacy of a destructive marriage
b. ambivalent separations— shattered dreams
c. traumatic separations— negative reconstructions

III. EXTERNAL–SOCIAL

a. tribal warfare
b. role of mental health professionals/attorneys
c. role of Court/Judge

F I G U R E   8 – 1

Sources of Divorce Impasses

Reprinted with permission of the
author, Janet R. Johnston.

The External-Social Network Level of Impasse

The easiest level to recognize is the outer, or "external-social network," level. Normally, people who get divorced turn to others—parents, other family members, close friends—for support during the divorce process. Those who subsequently reach an impasse often retain their support system long after the divorce. They may use it to confirm their judgment and to circulate an image of the former spouse that exaggerates personal flaws into horrendous character defects while ignoring good points. Spreading the image to those they rely on emotionally, including perhaps a new significant other, becomes a way of justifying and affirming the polarized reality they have created. The conflict may be confined to a few close, supportive people, but in some cases it may spread to the children's teachers, therapists, and day-care providers, to the next-door neighbor and to the people in the carpool—sometimes even to the local and national media.

The more people who are involved, the more the conflict takes on a life of its own. Ultimately, it calls into question the ability of the couple to heal and to parent the children together. A support system that has accepted the distorted image of the ex-spouse as true may no longer tolerate a resolution and the building of mutual respect and cooperation. The individual has locked himself or herself into, and perhaps become accountable to, a network that sanctions only punitive actions against the ex-spouse. Johnston and Campbell term construction of such an external social network "tribal warfare."[1]

Both legal and mental health professionals, unless they are fully aware, may inadvertently be pulled into this sort of warfare, exacerbating the conflict and deepening the impasse. Lawyers, expected to side with their clients and to act in what appear to be their clients' best interests, sometimes accept the involvement of numerous witnesses who publicly affirm the ex-spouse's bad character or poor parenting. The resulting escalation of conflict in a tense courtroom drama may hinder the prospects for cooperative parenting and, ultimately, hurt the client's children.

Therapists are prone to the same polarization process. In individual therapy, the therapist hears one parent's version of the relationship. This may draw well-meaning therapists into the external-social network. The distress of a client determined to be officially declared the only good parent may convince a naive therapist to testify in court that the other parent "cannot be trusted not to threaten and bully" and should have only limited or no visitation rights. A therapist may inadvertently further entrench a conflict and deepen the impasse.

The Interactional Level of Impasse

The next level at which an impasse may be imbedded and perpetuated is the interactional level. Here the impasse arises from the face-to-face transactions between the individuals. Impasses based on the couple's interactions generally represent conflicts that have roots in three areas.

The Destructive Legacy. The first area is the legacy of a truly destructive marriage. Couples in this group have had a very unhappy partnership. As individuals, many of them function fairly well—in their jobs, as parents, and in the community. When they are together, however, they create enormous difficulties for each other. Their barbs and criticisms seem calculated to engage each other's vulnerabilities and undo each other's defenses. All the contentious interactions of their marriage are mirrored in the divorce and carried into present interchanges.

The Sudden Abandonment. The second type of couple likely to reach an impasse at the interactional level are those whose marriages fall apart suddenly, without warning. One partner may have a love affair and leave abruptly, or one spouse may flee from what he or she perceives as danger or emotional abuse. The salient characteristic of these situations is their lack of an opportunity for closure, for a chance to talk it through, to hear and attempt to understand the causes of the separation. Instead, what remains is an enormous sense of betrayal. The abandoned spouse feels hurt and angry, totally focused on the deceit of the other person. Humiliation and rage make it extremely difficult to deal with the separation and begin the healing process so necessary for postdivorce adjustment.

The Ambivalent Separation. The third and final type of couple who often reach an impasse at the interactional level are experiencing an ambivalent separation. They may have met in a highly romantic fashion and had high hopes and dreams for their marriage. When one or both of them fail to live up to the other's fantasies or ideals, these couples often cycle through periods of intense arguments before finally disengaging from each other. When they meet again after the divorce, during mediation, or at exchanges of the children, they are prone to reromanticize the relationship. Forgetting their past inability to function as a couple, they may start to believe they can make it work again. When conflict returns—as it invariably does—it may become the passion that keeps them emotionally connected, albeit negatively. These kinds of couples do best if kept away from each other, both during mediation and on other co-parenting occasions.

The Intrapsychic Level of Impasse

The third area of impasse identified by Johnston and Campbell is the intrapsychic area.[1] People who fall into this category of impasse are predisposed by personality structure to experience serious problems in maintaining an intimate relationship. Their characterological limitations are present long before marriage but frequently do not emerge for some time. In fact, many such individuals project great personal magnetism and seem genuinely interested in other people. Over time, however, their ingrained personality style leads to the deterioration of many of their close relationships, including their marriage.

The characteristics of this personality structure—often referred to as a *disorder of the self*—are reflected in the individual's day-to-day functioning. They frequently lack empathy and the capacity of self-observation; therefore such people cannot project themselves into the place of others or understand how their actions affect others. As a group, they have no tolerance of emotional pain. Although they are often very vulnerable people, they rarely acknowledge to themselves or to others that something has hurt them. Having erected walls of denial around their pain, they express it as anger.

Their response is traceable to very early experiences. Most of them lacked good, solid models of parenting from their own childhoods. Often they grew up in abusive homes or in families that offered them little empathy or protection from emotional pain. Some grew up in families with unclear boundaries and little respect for individuality. As a result, these individuals cannot trust others, nor can they tolerate feelings of hurt; they cannot acknowledge their vulnerability and pain.

What is likely to happen when people with such characteristics enter the arena of divorce—where rejection, pain, and humiliation are almost always present? Part of the divorce process entails recognizing and working through pain. It necessitates pulling oneself up by one's bootstraps and reconstructing a self-image as a desirable, good person. Individuals unable to tolerate pain and rejection have no way to do this. They cannot grieve their losses, establish goals for new growth, and rebuild their lives. Because they cannot bear pain, they cover it with anger. Rigidly defending themselves from experiencing pain, they convert sadness into rage. As long as they can direct that rage toward an external object, they can avoid recognizing the pain within themselves.

Putting the Model Together

The particular nature of an impasse—the vulnerability and woundedness of the parents—must guide the design of an appropriate intervention strategy and co-parenting plan. In deciding which strategies to build into a plan, mental health or legal professionals will also need to keep in mind that the individual members of a couple exhibit different levels of woundedness, or subjective distress, at different times. The criteria spelled out on the Severity of Vulnerability Scale (Table 8–1), as well as the discussion which follows, will be helpful in assessing a given individual's level of vulnerability.

Woundedness is a concept defined by an interaction between (1) lifelong patterns of vulnerability and (2) marital and divorce injuries. *Vulnerability* is defined as those factors at the intrapsychic level that predispose certain people to conflict even before marriage and divorce. The unhappiness of the marital relationship (the interactional level) and the possible existence of tribal warfare after the divorce (the external-social network) constitute the injury, that is, what actually causes the individual to be hurt. The existence of these factors and their unique interaction are the signature of the impasse between any given couple.

Woundedness is a representation of the subjective distress people feel. If a person's vulnerability is high on the scale of severity (see Table 8–1), a relatively lesser composite of injuries can cause him or her high levels of subjective distress, or woundedness. A less vulnerable individual might well experience the same level of injuries with a lower level of woundedness, or subjective distress.

Levels of Vulnerability

As mentioned before, the predominant characteristic of people with intrapsychic problems is their refusal to experience and accept their own pain. Instead, they externalize it as anger and direct it toward others. Their inability to understand their own contribution to the marital breakup often leads them to conclude that the fault must lie outside themselves. Most frequently, the ex-spouse receives the brunt of the blame, although attorneys, custody evaluators, therapists, the court, or even the children themselves may come in for a share.

These individuals' limited capacity to empathize with others makes it tremendously difficult for them to protect their own

T A B L E 8 - 1
Severity of Vulnerability Scale

Criteria	Mild Traits							Ingrained Personality Structure
Will not experience pain, will not hurt, externalizes pain								
Cannot accept their own role in the breakup of marriage—no capacity for insight								
Cannot protect the children from the conflict; little awareness of or empathy for impact conflict has on children								
Degree of devaluing other parent								
Level of intensity								
Insatiable quality—nothing seems to resolve the conflict								
Time frame of conflict—how long at this level of intensity								
Pervasiveness across other social, emotional, and occupational relationships								
Active intensification of the conflict through recruitment of others								

children from interparental conflict. They tend to view their children not as separate individuals with separate needs but as extensions of themselves. Such parents cannot put themselves in their children's place to experience the unhappiness that divorce causes them.

When working with highly vulnerable people, parenting coordinators, attorneys, or ex-spouses frequently find that the principal task is keeping the focus of discussion on the children. Although they may begin by talking about the children, people of this type soon drift back to reciting the faults of their ex-spouse. By shifting the focus of discussion away from the children, they bring it back to impasse.

The intensity and longevity of their feelings are other indicators of a high level of vulnerability. Vulnerable people may be able to avoid the pain of divorce only by storing up anger; they dare not let go of it. Even two or three years after the divorce their animosity may be so great that they are incapable of saying even one good thing about the other parent. Individuals who continue to function at the high level of intensity ordinarily characteristic of only the first six months after divorce are showing signs of characterological disturbance.

Frequently these are focused and energetic people, seemingly tireless in recruiting others to their position. Many keep a mental record, if not a written one, enumerating the ex-spouse's inadequacies, culpabilities, and perceived transgressions. They may come to mediation or court meetings equipped with journals and notebooks documenting fifteen years of such transgressions committed against themselves, the children, or the community. Some file entries are mountains and others are molehills, but all are emblazoned in memory as well as recorded on paper.

These highly vulnerable people have worked hard to spread the conflict. The file may include official documents and copies of negative testimonials against the ex-spouse from others. Over time, the divorce impasse has been strengthened by sharing a disparaging view of the ex-spouse with others, who have subsequently reinforced and validated it.

Recognizing the High-Risk Individual

People displaying certain defensive styles are especially likely to be caught up in divorce impasse. These high-risk individuals share (1) an unwillingness or inability to experience the loss and rejection that are part of divorce and (2) a predisposition to project onto others the blame for the family breakup. We need not characterize such people by precise diagnostic labels because they frequently overlap categories and vary by intensity and duration, but they can easily be recognized by their manner and behavior. One group projects a sense of "I'm always right"; another seems to say, "You're always wrong"; and a third conveys a mixed message that can be described as "Maybe I will and maybe I won't." While there is likely to be some overlap of these characteristics, as well as some variability in degree of severity from person to person, nonetheless, each variation represents a maladaptive response to the pain of divorce.

One additional, and opposing, style of defense is sometimes adopted by an ex-spouse in response to one of the three styles of conflict initiation who initiate conflict. During marriage this sort of individual is highly dependent on his or her spouse. Although unlikely to initiate a conflict, he or she tends to perpetuate it by passive behavior and an inability to set limits on the other's demands. People in this group are usually characterized by high vulnerability and suffer a great deal of distress following a divorce. We characterize them as "the easy-to-victimize ex-spouse."

"I'm Always Right"

We refer to the first group of traits as "I'm always right," but there is more to this label. In full, it is "I'm always right and if you don't hear me the first time, I'll say it again, louder." It is characteristic of people in this group that their perception of reality is not altered by any argument presented to them. They are totally self-assured. In fact, they may be so unrealistically self-confident as to assert their superior judgment in areas in which they have no true expertise. Their unshakable beliefs—often formed in early childhood—tend to be self-righteous, self-aggrandizing, and self-serving. Individuals in this group cannot fathom the idea that another person does not agree with them. If others do not accede to their opinion, it must be because they have not heard or understood it properly. Hence, these people may state their opinion again, louder.

Such people may be viewed by others as fun-loving and socially adept. They are frequently attractive and draw people to them. Many are successful in professional, artistic, or commercial endeavors. Others may be somewhat grandiose in manner and project an air of entitlement. They may enjoy bestowing gifts, large and small, upon themselves. Nothing is too good for them, and no gesture or gift can sufficiently reflect their high merit. There may be a sense of being in the presence of royalty. Usually they have been functioning in this way since early childhood, perhaps modeling themselves on one of their parents or on another adult role model.

Sadly, many of these individuals experience a succession of failed relationships and may well have children from each of them. Instead of working through their problems with intimacy, they tend to blame their ex-spouse or other external causes and move on to a new relationship. Without insight into their own role in the last marriage's failure, but with a new set of expectations, they launch the next relationship. It may work for a while before foundering on the very same set of problems.

Divorce impasse in couples with one individual of this kind often results from his or her insistence on setting all the rules. These individuals feel that they are entitled to control decisions involving the children, even if their relationship with them is not close. For example, one couple, Megan and Jordan, parents of David, age five, needed to decide whether David would begin school in the fall. Because of his late-summer birthday, he would be one of the youngest children in his class if he started school that year. If he waited a year, he would be one of the oldest. Jordan researched the question with an educational consultant and discussed it with school counselors at both elementary- and middle-school levels. Finally, he spoke with David's therapist, who understood the problems the boy was having with peer relations and with feelings about his small physical stature. Perhaps because of being caught in numerous loyalty binds between angry parents, David also had difficulty concentrating and was easily distracted. The educational experts agreed that he would benefit from starting school a year later, when he had matured a bit more. Megan, however, insisted that he was ready for school that fall. Without consulting anyone, she instructed her lawyer to take the issue to court. As his mother, she asserted, she alone knew best what would be in her child's best interest.

Besides a succession of failed intimate relationships, people who use this defensive style frequently have a history of failed relationships with lawyers and therapists. They are likely to shop around until they find a professional who will buy into their point of view and support their self-serving views. If a lawyer or therapist challenges their judgment or fails to win a favorable decision in court, she or he is summarily fired and the parent moves on to a new, "more competent" professional.

Occasionally these individuals become violent, impulsively; they are unlikely to premeditate violence. Frequently they do, however, get into a cycle of spouse battering. An individual may be attracted to an "I'm always right" spouse because he or she projects tremendous self-confidence, as well as offering structure, rules, and a strong belief system. Such people appear to have all the answers. Some partners become passive-dependent over time; years of having their opinions and contributions belittled by an "I'm always right" spouse can undermine their sense of competency and self-esteem.

If, however, a couple like this reaches an impasse over some issue and the less assertive partner resists the point of view offered by the "I'm always right" spouse violence may erupt. An "I'm always right" person finds it extremely difficult to back down from a position. Although the violence is likely to be impulsive, as opposed to premeditated, in some relationships it becomes a recurrent pattern.

"You're (Ex-Spouse) Always Wrong"

The second defensive style highly predisposed to initiate divorce impasse is the "You're always wrong" style. These people may be intensely focused and very energetic. Like "I'm always right," people with this style have from early childhood organized their beliefs around specious or faulty notions that, by their adulthood, have become absolutely unshakable.

In contrast to the "I'm always right," however, "You're always wrong" traits are not often as likable. These people may project a focused intensity and a thinly veiled hostility that evoke fear or avoidance in others. Their anger may show through their unrelenting energy and overcontrolled, sometimes angry and sometimes emotionless, manner of speaking.

In a situation of divorce impasse they are prone to commit character assassination against the ex-spouse. They do so by picking out instances of objectionable behavior by him or her and making them public, often utilizing tribal warfare to spread the denigrating view. They may go through professional relationships in quick succession, firing any attorney or therapist who challenges their firm belief that the ex-spouse is an undesirable and incompetent parent. They have a deep memory of offenses committed by the ex-spouse and may bury professionals in heaps of documents detailing all of them.

The overcontrolling personality of these individuals and their fear that they may lose control of their impulses may provoke their spouses to make a sudden move to escape from the relationship. During divorce and mediation proceedings, overcontrolling partners may play on their ex-spouses' impulsiveness by goading them into sudden expressions of hostility while they remain calm and apparently unperturbed. People who use this style may be capable of premeditating violence or of provoking violence in their spouses.

In a divorce impasse, individuals of this group may well reiterate the ex-spouse's responsibility for all problems. Even when they begin to discuss the children's issues, they may focus the discussion back on the offenses of the ex-spouse. Attempts to contradict or temper this judgment with contrary evidence are not likely to succeed. Expert opinions, judges' orders, documented research findings, and the positive testimonials of others—all have no effect. They continue to believe unshakably that "You're always wrong."

One way to deal with these individuals around co-parenting issues is to say something like, "Obviously, I'm not going to shake you out of that position [the guiltiness and culpability of the ex-spouse], but we're not here to debate that issue. Let's focus instead on how you are going to co-parent. That's what we're here to discuss." In this way, the mediator or parenting coordinator takes the defenses into account but does not attempt to confront them directly.

In extreme cases, individuals of this character style may stalk their ex-spouse and may commit premeditated crimes of violence against them, the court, the attorneys, and others involved in the case. Some may be capable of restricting their extreme expressions of hostility to the former spouse; others, however, are involved in chronic conflict on the job and in the community.

"Maybe I Will and Maybe I Won't"

The third style of defense likely to initiate divorce impasse is the "Maybe I will and maybe I won't" style. The full label of this style is "Maybe I will and maybe I won't, and probably I'll run out of the room and slam the door behind me." These are people who have a great deal of difficulty containing their rage. A very small provocation may put them in touch with it. Their anger is so easily triggered and so unpredictable that others feel they have to "walk on eggshells" around them.

They find it very difficult to see two sides of a conflict and cannot tolerate even minor rejections or criticisms. They focus a great deal on loyalty issues. People must be either for them all the way or it is assumed that others are against them. If they are challenged, even on one small point, they may feel totally betrayed. They sometimes display a pattern of dropping their friends one by one, becoming progressively more socially isolated and accusing former friends of disloyalty. Unfortunately, their own children are at some risk of also falling into this pattern of condemnation and rejection.

It is difficult to keep such individuals focused on one task at a time. They are highly impulsive and may appear at times to scatter their energy with no clear direction, feeling at home in the midst of disorder. Wherever they go, lack of clarity and a confusion about which rules they are playing by follow them. Because they so easily infuse with rage, it may be difficult for them to focus clearly. They may start off talking about one topic, but before they have finished it they have moved on to another. They may be illogical at times and may lose their train of thought in mid-sentence. On these occasions, they may become fast talkers, mixing fantasy or fabrication with reality to justify their arguments.

An example of this behavior was given by Amy, a young mother of a preschooler, during a segment of a co-parenting session held to set the agenda of topics for discussion. As soon as a topic was mentioned, she would experience a flood of emotion, a racing of ideas, and a press to discuss the issue fully. When another subject was introduced, she would jump to it, expressing a largely incoherent jumble of ideas and accusations. She had to be reminded repeatedly that the first order of business of the meeting was to set an agenda and that the various issues would be discussed fully later in the meeting. Like many other people who use the "Maybe I will and maybe I won't" style, she appeared to be acting under her own set of rules. No matter how clearly the rules were spelled out, she interpreted them in her own way.

Another hallmark of the "Maybe I wills" is their inability to share the children. They seem to need to feel in total control or not in control at all. Very often these individuals either had sole care of the children during the marriage or participated only minimally. When locked in divorce conflict, they frequently insist on changing the co-parenting rules unilaterally in order to feel in control. If forced to share control, they may threaten to actually drop out of the children's lives, blaming external circumstances—the legal system, the ex-spouse, and others—

for their own inability to stay involved with the children on a shared basis.

They thus have a great deal of difficulty making and keeping agreements. Disappointing others' expectations seems to give them a sense of control. No matter what arrangements have been made, these individuals will not carry them out as expected. If they even come close to obeying someone else's rules, they feel they will lose their self-identity and independence. When another person manages to exercise an equal degree of authority, they will often pull back.

Yet they must also maintain a balance. Since early childhood these individuals have experienced a disturbing dilemma in regard to intimate relationships: if others pull back too far, they may feel abandoned: if others come too close, they will feel smothered. Their underlying fear of being engulfed—in essence, annihilated—by another person and losing their identity has deep roots. At the same time a friend, lover, or family member who seems too cool and distant can trigger feelings of abandonment. A frequent defense against such a possibility is rejecting the other person first (that is, abandoning others), enacting the very behavior they fear the most.

People with this style are at risk of becoming self-destructive as well. The "Maybe I will, maybe I won't" shares with the "I'm always rights" and the "You're always wrongs" a proneness to project their anger by acting out against others or their property. However, they are also capable of turning their anger against themselves. They may threaten suicide and sometimes carry out the gesture as a means of control or manipulation. In the worst-case scenario, they commit suicide, the ultimate abandonment of those they perceive as abandoning them.

Because of this personality structure, they function in a very narrow social range that makes co-parenting exceedingly difficult. Mental health and legal professionals dealing with these people must first recognize their defensive structure and hear their message of "Come closer/Back away." There are bound to be many instances of disappointed expectations and difficulties in reaching agreement. For their children, the risk of failing to keep them involved is condemnation, accusation, or abandonment. When these parents do drop out, they are very likely to blame others: their lawyer, the legal system, the ex-spouse, the weather. They may even—worst of all—blame the children for their own withdrawal from or inability to share parental responsibilities.

"Easy-to-Victimize Ex-Spouses"

People with the three coping styles described above are likely to be the initiators of conflict. By shielding themselves from the emotional distress of the failed marriage and placing the blame on their ex-spouses, they can avoid acknowledging their own contribution. All of these types are likely to select spouses whose high dependency needs make them easy to victimize. This fourth group of high-risk individuals can, therefore, be described as "easy-to-victimize ex-spouses."

These sometimes passive and compliant individuals keep the conflict going through their inability to set limits on the demands of the ex-spouse. As children, people with this coping style were often severely criticized, humiliated, shamed, and/or abused by a powerful parent. One father caught in a divorce impasse revealed that he could never win the approval of his own critical father. Even when he was selected by the optimists as "student of the year," his father disparaged the achievement with these cutting words: "You may be able to fool all of them, but I know who you really are." A continuous barrage of such insidious psychological abuse induces self-doubt and undermines the self-confidence of the individuals subjected to it. They come to doubt the validity of their own ideas and emotions and to look outside themselves for a structure and a belief system that will gain them approval.

Sadly, some of these people are attracted to dominating people such as those with "I'm always right" traits. They may even be exploited by the rigid ideologies and charismatic personalities of extremist cult leaders. In a marital or other intimate relationship they are apt to be genuinely confused about their own responsibility for the hurtful behavior of a partner who exudes certainty and self-confidence. Many struggle with poor self regard and speak of themselves in a self-deprecating manner. Even after divorce, they may continue to accept the blame when things go wrong. Along with the ex-spouse, they are their own harshest critics. Their anger tends to be expressed indirectly, if at all, sometimes in a passive-aggressive interpersonal style.

For them, the divorce brings back self-doubts they may have kept buried during the marriage. They may see themselves as doomed to fail and experience the loss of the spouse as proof of their lack of personal competence and attractiveness. Even if they begin to build feelings of self-respect and independence, their problems may continue. A demanding ex-spouse who is accustomed to having his or her demands adhered to will probably feel the former "victim's" newfound, positive self-esteem as a challenge and may intensify the conflict.

Creating a Parenting Plan

As we have reiterated throughout the book, the goal of co-parenting is the reduction of interparental conflict for the benefit of the children. Although custody and visitation arrangements are specified in final divorce decrees, not all divorced parents are capable of carrying them out cooperatively. While some couples use the legal arena to resolve disputes, others seek the assistance of therapists, and still others attempt mediation.

In recent years mediation has been recognized as an effective means of reducing conflict at the time of the divorce. It has not, however, been shown to be successful in facilitating long-term co-parenting. It has not been set up to deal with the complicated social network, interpersonal factors, and interactional dynamics that characterize high-conflict divorce. Nor has mediation been employed as a means to protect the children from long-term divorce issues. A mediator or arbitrator in some joint-custody situations or a Guardian *ad litem* in other custody situations may perform these functions, but in many high-conflict divorces, no professional is officially appointed. We feel this professional role is in need of further definition, clarification, and training in effective techniques and approaches.

We propose defining this role as *parenting coordinator*. He or she will carry out a twofold function: (1) translating the visitation plan into a conflict-reduction plan tailored specifically to the dynamics of the divorce impasse and (2) assisting parents to implement it on an ongoing basis. In the remainder of this chapter we will discuss the first function; Chapter 9 will describe in detail the second of these two tasks.

A parenting coordinator will need to be experienced in several different disciplines: problem resolution, mediation techniques, communications, and the legal aspects of divorce, as well as adult psychotherapy, developmental psychology, and children's adjustment issues that are specific to divorce.

In the ideal situation, a parenting coordinator would be brought in as soon as it is clear that a high degree of conflict between parents is affecting the children. This may be early in the divorce process, when the parenting coordinator can assume a mediating role in helping establish the residence and visitation plan. If parents fail to reach a decision at that point, it may be necessary to bring in an outside custody evaluator. The parenting coordinator should not move into the role of custody evaluator. Making the decision to place the child in the residence and custody of one of the parents would seriously compromise his or her neutrality.

In other cases, a parenting coordinator may be appointed after the custody evaluation has been completed. In fact, the custody evaluation might well designate a coordinator to implement and maintain the residence and visitation plan. Finally, a parenting coordinator should remain an option at any point after the divorce for parents who continue to fight and relitigate.

The parenting coordinator would have the following broad responsibilities:

1. Creating a parenting plan to contain or reduce interparental conflict
2. Ensuring execution of the residence and visitation ar-

rangements specified in the divorce decree or in temporary orders

3. Monitoring visitation and mediating disputes between parents
4. Teaching parents communication skills, principles of child development, and children's issues in divorce
5. Exercising the power to modify visitation as a means of reducing conflict
6. Ensuring that both parents maintain ongoing relationships with the children
7. Acting as arbitrator (that is, final decision maker) on any issue over which the parents reach an impasse

Some divorced parents require a great deal of co-parenting help to minimize conflict; others need only an occasional tie-breaker. In Table 8–2, we detail the roles a parenting coordinator might play when different degrees of interparental conflict are present. At all levels, the primary aim of the parenting coordinator will be to help parents develop strategies for (1) parenting in a manner that minimizes conflict; (2) disengaging from each other; and (3) allowing the children to grow up free from the threat of being caught in the middle of their parents' disputes.

It is especially important for the parenting coordinator to be capable of recognizing couples who are at high risk of remaining in long-term conflict. As we pointed out earlier, half of all divorcing couples who are in moderate to high conflict during the first year of divorce will probably still be clashing three or four years later.

Moreover, research indicates that couples rarely move directly from conflictual to cooperative parenting; they almost always need to go through the intermediate step of disengagement.[2] If the members of a couple can first learn to disengage from each other, they will often be able to parent cooperatively at a later date. The process of disengagement is easier for some divorcing parents than for others. Those most likely to be successful generally have low vulnerability and have sustained only mild to moderate degrees of woundedness during the mar-

T A B L E   8 - 2
Role of Parenting Coordinator

	Level of Conflict	
Minimal/Mild	Moderate	Moderately Severe/Severe
Ultimate decision maker and tiebreaker	Teaches models of communication	Full-time coordinator officially appointed in final divorce decree
Adjusts visitation according to changing developmental needs	Educates around parenting skills	Adapts communication techniques to nature of impasse
Adjusts visitation according to changing external circumstances	Modifies visitation to minimize conflict	Modifies visitation to minimize conflict
Meets with both parents only when needed	Assists in developing low-conflict drop-off and pickup plans	Recommends supervised visitation when necessary for child's protection
	Mediates agreements regarding joint or sole attendance at school and recreational events	Recommends full evaluation of one or both parents when necessary (i.e., alcohol use, substance abuse, severe psychopathology)
	Troubleshoots problem areas in visitation plan that impact on children	Ensures child will have contact with both parents
	Meets at 1- to 3-month intervals, more often if necessary	Devises and arranges for implementation of visitation and communication plan for parental alienation
		Meets as often as necessary—typically once a week

riage and divorce. The Severity of Vulnerability Scale (Table 8–1) can be used to identify each parent's susceptibility to high-conflict co-parenting.

Before creating the parenting plan, therefore, the coordinator will need to meet with the couple to assess their vulnerability and woundedness and the external social factors. The principal goal of this meeting is the identification of each person's potential triggers for defensiveness. This step should be omitted if this information is already available in a custody and visitation evaluation.

The parenting coordinator may elect to see the couple jointly —to observe their communication style, level of negative affect and the defensiveness between them—or individually. If mutual hostility is extremely high or impulse control is in doubt (for example, if there is a history or threat of violence), joint meetings will probably heighten conflict and may serve no useful purpose.

When the parenting coordinator has identified the couple's risk for continued conflict, he or she will be prepared to create a parenting plan that takes that risk into account. Within the framework of its primary goal—minimizing the children's exposure to conflict—the plan will be designed to achieve a balance between the children's developmental needs and fair and reasonable parental time-sharing. Using his or her knowledge of the parents' defensive strategies, the parenting coordinator will draft a plan that, rather than confronting these defenses and activating the pain underlying them, works around them.

We have seen, for example, that each of the three conflict-initiators described in the preceding section uses a different defensive strategy for self-protection from pain. The self-aggrandizing parents who utilize to the "I'm always right" strategy—with their predisposition to grandiosity and aura of entitlement—shield themselves from pain by believing in their own infallibility. The "You're always wrongs" exclude awareness of their own role in the marital failure by focusing on the ex-spouse's inability to live up to some personal set of standards of parenting. The defenses of the "Maybe I will and maybe I won't," by contrast, are confused and shifting. These people protect themselves from pain by refusing to commit to a firm position, remaining moving targets and avoiding accountability for their own behavior. Finally, although it seems like no defense at all, the defense of the "easy-to-victimize ex-spouse" is dependency. In essence, depending on the approval of others and projecting an air of inadequacy forces others to bear all the responsibility for the marital failure and its accompanying suffering.

The parenting coordinator's knowledge of the parents' defenses can help him or her serve an educative and redirecting role. Attempting to build self-awareness on the part of either or both parents may not be as effective an approach. Using behavioral strategies and cognitive reframing techniques to achieve the primary goal of protecting the children from loyalty binds and exposure to conflict often succeeds far better. These techniques and some specific strategies for dealing with each of the above four defensive styles are discussed in detail in Chapter 9.

When the parenting coordinator has assessed the defensive styles, individual personality characteristics, and interactional dynamics of the couple, he or she will create a highly detailed and specific parenting plan. This is not the same as a visitation plan. The goal of a parenting plan is to minimize the factors that produce conflict so as to ensure smooth implementation of the visitation plan. Issues that are not typically addressed by custody evaluators or by a court-mandated visitation plan are detailed in written form. The parenting plan would deal with such matters as:

1. Communication between parents
2. Arrangements for dropping off and picking up the children
3. Parents' attendance at school and recreational events
4. Agreements about telephone contacts between parents and between children and parents
5. Sharing of children's toys and other possessions between the two homes
6. Methods of resolving disputes

7. Flexibility in scheduling, if allowed
8. Handling children's refusal to visit
9. Emergency procedures for unexpected interparental flare-ups

A comprehensive parenting plan including these and other arrangements for contingencies will be developed, put into written form, and distributed to both parents, both sets of attorneys, the court, and all therapists involved with the children and the adults. The plan will involve agreements based on a set of rules for visitation, communication, and dispute resolution devised to minimize the parents' triggers for conflict. It will also educate each parent about the other's potential triggers and provide specific recommendations for communicating and interacting in a way that is less likely to cause arguments. These recommendations cannot, of course, be enforced as visitation rules can be. However, impressing parents repeatedly, and in several different contexts, of the critical importance of minimizing conflict and avoiding its detrimental effects on their children can be helpful toward its enforcement over time. (See the sample Parenting Plan and Parenting Checklist in Appendix A and Appendix B.)

In helping to implement the parenting plan, one of the coordinator's major roles is maintaining communication among all parties by serving as a conduit for information. Confidentiality may or may not be an effective tool of the parenting coordinator. Unlike a therapist, a parenting coordinator is not the ally of either parent; nor is he or she a neutral mediator. The coordinator's role is a more active one specifically focused on helping parents work together for the benefit of their children. Whatever specific task is being performed—educating parents in techniques for co-parenting, building their insight and communication skills, interviewing the children and/or other professionals involved with them, or tiebreaking (arbitrating)—the parenting coordinator's one fundamental aim is to minimize the conflict to which the children are exposed.

The relationship between the children and each parent is the coordinator's client. Sometimes the task of structuring the children's environment to minimize conflict calls for acting in a therapeutic manner toward the parents. Even then, however, the ultimate concern must remain the children. Professionals who in the past have functioned as therapists, custody evaluators, and mediators will need to rethink their role. To be a successful parenting coordinator they will need to draw on all these areas of expertise. As we will see in Chapter 9, implementing a parenting plan requires a unique synthesis of strategy and action.

9

Implementing the Parenting Plan

Parents vary considerably in their ability to carry out a parenting plan. In general, a couple's need for ongoing help from the parenting coordinator depends on how successfully they can disengage from one another, and thus, lower the level of mutual conflict. The nature and frequency of access to the coordinator that a particular couple will need, therefore, are determined by their level of conflict—minimal to mild, moderate, or moderately severe to severe (as represented in Table 8–2). While those in the first category may require only minimal contact—perhaps only once every three months plus occasional meetings to arbitrate disputes—couples in moderately severe to severe conflict usually need to meet with the coordinator at least weekly.

At all levels of conflict, one of the principal functions of the parenting coordinator is to help resolve disputes as a tie-breaker, or arbitrator. In these cases, both parents must agree beforehand to abide by the decision. After giving both parents ample opportunity to present their sides of the issue, the coordinator will make the decision and present it in written form—to avoid miscommunication and misinterpretation.

In addition to resolving disputes, the parenting coordinator for parents in minimal to mild conflict will probably be called upon from time to time to modify the visitation plan. All possible changes in a family's circumstances cannot, of course, be foreseen when the plan is originated. A parent may move his or her residence or change jobs. When parents remarry, as most do within five years of divorce, they create new living arrangements as well as new family dynamics. Visitation plans may also need to be adjusted to children's changing developmental needs, new schools, or evolving outside interests. The parenting coordinator will therefore need to remain accessible to all parents—even those who can co-parent successfully with only mild or occasional conflict—on an as-needed basis.

As we have seen earlier, couples who remain in moderate conflict often function well as individuals but are very prone to trigger each other's defenses when they meet. Often they favor a flexible visitation plan, only to find that their negative interactional style makes them incapable of negotiating such issues as trading weekends or rescheduling pickup times. Their interactions at drop-off and pickup times, when they need to communicate information about their children's needs and schedules, are likely to be tense and to escalate easily into open hostilities. Over time, these parents often become so sensitive to each other's faultfinding that they experience almost any comment as an insult or a criticism.

To save their children from the inevitable loyalty binds created by these encounters, a couple in moderate conflict will require a more structured co-parenting plan and more intervention by the coordinator than mild- to minimal-conflict parents. Disputes requiring the parenting coordinator to act as a tiebreaker will erupt more frequently. The coordinator will need to devise a model for interparental communication and interaction and practice it with the couple. If parenting skills are lacking, the coordinator will need to work with one or both parents in learning them. These parents are likely also to need help in developing plans to share their children's schedules and possessions.

The fundamental need of couples at this and higher levels of conflict is disengagement from each other. The less direct contact they have with each other, the better. Although many will want to institute a cooperative and flexible parenting arrangement, they will, in fact, require strategies that minimize interparental contact and communications. A neutral drop-off place, for example, can provide the children with a calm transition from one home to the other. A journal or log may be passed between the adults as the children are exchanged and can substitute for oral communications about scheduled appointments, mealtimes, or medication needs. Joint attendance at children's school performances or sporting events is generally unwise, unless structured ahead of time to ensure that the parents will be kept separate. If joint attendance creates a loyalty bind for the children, as it frequently does, an agreement to split these special events will be required to keep the peace. Many of these are necessary interim measures until emotional disengagement between the former spouses is attained.

Couples in moderate conflict will benefit greatly from learning to parent at a distance. While guiding them toward disengagement through arbitration, educative efforts, and visitation strategies that reduce contact, the parenting coordinator will support them in rebuilding their lives as separate individuals. In the first year or two the coordinator will serve as a buffer, absorbing the impact of conflict and shielding the children from it. Within a year or two of taking the vital step of emotional disengagement, however, many couples will be able to move toward parenting cooperatively with only mild conflict.

In the meantime, as conflict can arise at unpredictable times and in unexpected ways, parents and children will need ready access to the coordinator. Nonetheless, the parameters of that access should be defined in advance, and couples in moderate conflict should be encouraged not to call the coordinator as crises arise. The goal is to help them to develop strategies for reducing conflict and to learn either to solve their own problems or to delay impulsive expressions of anger until the next co-parenting meeting.

Couples in moderately severe or severe conflict present the greatest challenge to a parenting coordinator. One or both parents at this level are likely to have some characterological problems or other disorder that threatens the children's emotional or physical well-being. The risk of parental alienation requires frequent and regular contact with a parenting coordinator. Spouse battering, physical and sexual abuse of children, after assessment and treatment planning, may require regular contact with a parenting coordinator as well. Moreover, the latter must be prepared to intervene in a possible emergency and may have to decide whether to call in police or social service officials. In these cases, it is essential to clarify well in advance of any possible need the basis on which the coordinator can be available to parents and children, as well as the limitations of the parenting coordinator role.

As emphasized in the chapters dealing with visitation and parental alienation, the critical goal of the parenting coordinator is to ensure the safety of the children during visitation. He or she must be capable of recognizing situations that endanger the children and of taking action to secure supervised visitation to safeguard them. At the least, it may be necessary to bring in a mental health professional trained in the specific area of risk—such as alcoholism, substance abuse, or violence—to assess a doubtful situation.

A parenting coordinator may not be skilled in psychological assessment or may not wish to impair his or her neutrality by performing such an evaluation personally. For this reason, the co-parenting agreement should stipulate that the coordinator can arrange for an outside evaluation as he or she sees fit. (See the sample Parenting Coordinator Agreement in Appendix C.) If the coordinator decides that the children should also be assessed, permission will have to be secured from the custodial parent or, in cases of joint legal custody, both parents.

Based on the evaluations of the relevant family members, the parenting coordinator will decide whether to institute supervised visitation to protect the children. The decision to move gradually from supervised to unsupervised visitation will also rest with the parenting coordinator.

In cases of parental alienation—as described fully in Chapters 6 and 7—the coordinator plays a unique role in helping to rebuild the parent–child relationship and to heal the children's refusal to visit one parent. In these cases, he or she may decide to supervise personally the visits between the children and the targeted parent. These sessions will provide opportunities to observe parent–child interactions firsthand, to teach relationship-building skills, and to judge the children's progress toward learning to trust and to feel emotionally safe with the targeted parent. These sessions can also help the coordinator reach decisions about unsupervised visitation or about increasing the time the children will spend with the targeted parent.

Impasse Intervention Techniques

In creating the parenting plan, as explained in Chapter 8, the primary goal of ensuring the children's safe, ongoing contact with both parents is best achieved by tailoring specific provisions to the parents' level of conflict. The methods of implementing the plan, however, also need to be geared to the nature of the divorce impasse and to the parental defensive styles described in Chapter 8 and illustrated in Figure 9–1. A parenting assessment conducted prior to designing the plan will help the coordinator to clarify the nature and intensity of these parental characteristics. This may be done by the parenting coordinator meeting directly with the children, by a review of a previous custody evaluation or by interviewing professionals previously involved with the family members.

Once a visitation plan has been structured, the parenting coordinator's chief goal will be to develop and teach adaptive techniques for contact and communication between the parents. Using behavioral techniques and cognitive reframing strategies suited to the parents' defensive styles has been shown to be far more effective in reducing conflict than short-term mediation, direct confrontation, or efforts to build insight through therapy.[1]

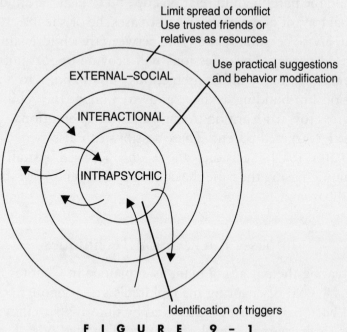

FOR ALL THREE LEVELS STAY FOCUSED ON THE CHILD
Use Cognitive Reframing Strategies

Limit spread of conflict
Use trusted friends or
relatives as resources

EXTERNAL–SOCIAL

Use practical suggestions
and behavior modification

INTERACTIONAL

INTRAPSYCHIC

Identification of triggers

F I G U R E   9 – 1
Impasse Intervention Techniques
Adapted from *Sources of Divorce Impasse*
by Janet Johnston, with permission.

The adaptive techniques we recommend are based on four broad strategies, three of which correspond to the sources of divorce impasse exhibited by the couple (see Figure 9–1). The first, overarching strategy for all sources of impasse is to keep the parents focused on the children at all times by using cognitive reframing strategies. The second strategy is designed specifically for couples whose impasse stems from their severe vulnerability (that is, the intrapsychic level of the impasse). For these parents, the parenting coordinator's primary task is identifying the triggers of conflict and teaching ways to minimize them. The third strategy utilizes a combination of behavior modification and practical suggestions for couples whose impasse is at the interactional level. The fourth focuses on limiting the spread of conflict that is centered on an external-social network.

Using Cognitive and Reframing Strategies to Stay Focused on the Child

We have identified the techniques in this category as cognitive strategies, that is, techniques that produce changes in behavior by deepening parents' understanding and perspective. It is, in fact, a mixed category. It includes both direct cognitive techniques—for example, teaching parenting skills—and behavioral approaches such as using the structural elements of the co-parenting plan as vehicles for inducing changes in behavior.

Educational Approach. All the cognitive and reframing strategies involve an effort to educate parents about the sources of their conflict and its effect on their children. When using a direct educative approach, the parenting coordinator identifies the areas of impasse that affect the parents' ability to co-parent cooperatively. It is essential, for example, for both parents to understand what constitutes a loyalty bind for their children and how it affects them. When a loyalty bind is identified as occurring, the coordinator will point it out and help the couple to deal with it in a new way allowing the child to succeed. It is important to help both parents acknowledge the relevance of the other parent to the children's lives and understand the serious emotional consequences of losing a parent. The coordinator will need to explain clearly, and perhaps repeatedly, that children who lose a parent early in life have problems with self-esteem that may last a lifetime. Why, these children question, did their mom or dad not love them enough to stay involved in their lives?

Structure of Parenting Meetings. Another important context for changes at the cognitive level is the parenting meeting. The structure of these sessions—who will attend them and how frequently and regularly they will be held—will need to be considered as well. For example, holding joint meetings for couples with a history of violence will almost certainly be stressful and needs to be determined on a case by case basis.

As discussed earlier in this chapter, the frequency of meetings will vary according to the level of conflict. While the parenting agreement is being drawn up, it will probably be necessary to hold meetings frequently; usually one-hour meetings once a week will suffice for drafting the agreement. In the implementation phase, except in cases of moderately severe or severe conflict, meetings can usually be cut back to once a month. If conflict flares up more often, the coordinator may decide to leave open the option of scheduling meetings on an as-needed basis. As couples learn strategies for managing their conflict, they can cut back on the frequency of meetings, depending on the age of the children. Parents of preschoolers can usually meet no more than once every six months, while families with school-age children may get together once a year—typically in the spring—to make summer plans and modify arrangements for the coming school year.

The parenting agreement needs to specify these matters of scheduling very carefully. It is all too easy for one member of a high-conflict couple to weaken the co-parenting process by claiming that he or she does not have either the time or the money to attend a session. One way to avoid the objection of a full calendar is to block out in advance all the possible times, week by week, when everyone can attend meetings if they become necessary. Establishing a posted retainer to pay for parenting sessions, which can then be drawn against as needed, may also make it easier to schedule meetings.

Finally, the parenting coordinator will need to identify who should attend a given session. Researchers Johnston and Campbell have described mediation sessions attended by stepparents, grandparents, or other extended family.[1] In some cases, the presence of these other people may keep an impulsive, scattered, or angry parent focused on problem solving; in others, however, the other parent may feel outnumbered and uncomfortable in such a session.

Principles of Time Sharing. It is not safe to assume that the parents will agree on the general principles of co-parenting and sharing their children. It is essential, therefore, to discuss explicitly certain basic principles of time-sharing. Four of the most important are that (1) both parents' houses will be home for the children; therefore, the children will have two families as well as two homes; (2) one parent will not dictate the rules to be followed in the other parent's household; (3) if possible, each parent will parent on some weekdays and some weekends; and (4) at certain times, siblings will move between households together, while at others they may go back and forth individually.

Identifying Shared Values. Identifying all the areas of philosophy and values shared by the parents can sometimes engender a spirit of cooperation. Often parents who have been locked in an impasse for a long time report that they disagree about everything. Upon examination, however, most realize that they agree about a surprising number of the values that made them select each other as partners in the first place. It often helps couples to identify these issues and write them down so they can see that even though their marriage is over, they still have purposes in common. Even agreeing about something as simple as regulating their children's television viewing—although each household may do so in its own way—can contribute a positive dimension to a co-parenting relationship.

Implementing Decisions with the Children. Discussing how to implement new parenting decisions and anticipating how they will affect children are important aspects of learning to co-parent. During parenting sessions both parents should endorse agreements and consider carefully the best ways of presenting them to the children. Parents who themselves understand the benefits of a parenting decision will also be better able to explain how the children will gain from it.

Some children of high-conflict divorce, particularly adolescents, have seized control for themselves during the months or years of interparental squabbling. They may well respond to their parents' suddenly joining forces and setting limits on them with suspicion and, quite possibly, rebellion. A parent who presents the new agreement without fully endorsing it can encourage such a reaction. For example, John, a father who had had difficulty setting limits for his troubled teenage son in the past, told the boy about a new agreement worked out in the parenting meeting: "Well, you know, I had to agree because otherwise I was going to be taken to court over this, but I do not really think much of the new time-sharing agreement. It is just another example of your mother's controlling everything." Clearly, this father was perpetuating a loyalty bind. Children who are repeatedly caught in such binds may become masters of manipulation, identifying their parents' triggers and reactivating conflict to escape the limits of a new rule.

Utilizing the Children's Input. A related question of co-parenting is how parents arrive at decisions that meet the needs of all family members and effectively enforce them. While children's input will be sought and thoughtfully considered, final decisions will be made by the parents, in consultation with the parenting coordinator. Frequently, rebellious adolescents and even some younger children will test the parents' capacity to follow through. Most children, however, report feeling relieved when both parents have the same expectations. Setting a time frame for trying out new visitation arrangements before adopting them as firm can be a helpful tool.

Understanding Parenting as an Ongoing Process. It is essential for parents to understand at the outset of the process that parenting, especially the co-parenting of young children, takes time to establish and will continue for many years. Often parents involved in a divorce impasse are impulsive people. They may expect to arrive at instantaneous, total, and forever solutions in one or two meetings and become impatient when there are no concrete results even after two or three parenting sessions. At the outset, the coordinator will need to set a realistic time frame, explaining that rebuilding parent–child relationships or establishing them for the first time may be a process of slowly increasing parenting and parental responsibility. As relationships are not fixed but grow and evolve over time, phasing in changes gradually helps maintain predictability and balance for children and parents as well.

For some parents, the parameters of a parental relationship are being defined for the very first time. Using the parenting agreement to delineate the positive contingencies of the parents' actions can help them adhere to its terms. For example, a father who has done very little parenting in the past may be willing and able. Agreeing to give him gradually increasing amounts of responsibility and time with the children as he masters effective parenting may provide an incentive. In such an instance the coordinator will be sure that both parents understand that "parenting" involves maintaining schedules, getting children to appointments on time, keeping up with schoolwork and after-school activities, and other practical responsibilities.

Parenting also means providing consistent affection and establishing a sense of safety and protection. Where one or both parents' history puts these matters in doubt, it is helpful to write into the agreement an explicit clause to cover possible negative contingencies, such as: "If there is continued use of alcohol, we agree to go to an alcohol treatment program accompanied by a temporary suspension of visits, followed by supervised visits, followed by monitored visits." Such a provision will make it clear that certain behavior may undermine the evolving relationship and set it back.

Establishing Communication Guidelines for the Parents. An extremely important aspect of maintaining an agreement successfully is parents' understanding of the detailed guidelines or rules for communication. Once these guidelines have been clearly defined, it is helpful to practice them during parenting sessions. The hope is that the newly established communication pattern will also be applied to interparental interactions occurring outside the meetings. These guidelines should include not interrupting, clearly distinguishing the issues from each other at the beginning of the session, and discussing those issues fully one at a time until they are resolved.

Except during parenting meetings, some couples will have to communicate with each other in writing. In cases of very high conflict, the parenting coordinator will review their letters before mailing them. The agreement should delineate all the graduated steps to be followed toward more normalized communication as these couples make progress in communicating clearly. For example, when they improve, they may write to each other directly, providing copies to the parenting coordinator. In the next step, they might write letters without sending copies to the coordinator. Ultimately, they may be able to talk to each other directly on the telephone or by voice recorders. Whatever the specific guidelines for interparental communication, they need to be clearly defined and understood.

Operationalizing Terms. In both designing and implementing a co-parenting plan, it is important to define concepts in terms of specific behavior. There will be fewer areas for misinterpretation and possible later disagreement about expectations if, for example, terms such as *invasion of privacy* and *violation of interpersonal boundaries* are concretely defined. It will be necessary to explain such phrases as "taking complete responsibility for the children on your scheduled time" in terms of discrete behaviors.

Sometimes a concept that seems self-evident, such as "no fighting in front of the children," may be clear to one parent but not to the other. For example, Will, a father in high conflict with his ex-spouse, believed he was not fighting in front of the children. Randy, the mother, claimed he was. Will maintained that as the children were in the next room, they were not fighting *in front of them,* even though the children could hear everything their parents said to each other. This couple clearly required guidelines written at a very specific level, including: "Do not speak to each other at the time of exchange"; "Do not share legal documents with the children"; "Do not discuss with the children your suspicion that their mother is plotting to remove them from their father's care"; "Do not attempt to answer children's questions about their mother's motivation but redirect them to her for an explanation of her behavior, and she will do the same for you." A parenting coordinator helping such parents draw up an agreement may need to start at one level of specificity, later revising its terms to higher levels as problems of interpretation indicate that concepts may still be too abstract.

Identifying the Triggers for Personality Style Impasse

Although each individual has his or her own areas and issues that induce anger, certain triggers are inherent in the four coping styles we discussed in Chapter 8. Identifying the situations that trigger a parent's anger and lead to an escalation of interparental conflict is a necessary first step in developing strategies to deal with these situations.

"I'm Always Right." Individuals who adopt the "I'm always right" style react with anger to various kinds of situations. One of these is passive-aggressive behavior on the part of the exspouse. When a decision is made, he or she expects the exspouse to adhere to it strictly. Any testing of the limits of an agreement feels like undermining it completely. Frequently the overdominant style of the "I'm always right" person leads a passive-aggressive or passive-dependent ex-spouse to be reluctant to bring up lesser issues for discussion. Yet it is important for this ex-spouse to recognize that—as any deviation from the agreement will trigger high-conflict behavior—it is better in the long run to raise even what appear to be small or insignificant issues beforehand. If, for example, a parent agrees in writing to take the child to soccer practice every other Wednesday, it is important to do so. The "I'm always right" person is very unlikely to greet with flexibility or understanding an ex-spouse's rearrangements, no matter how sensible or well reasoned.

By the same token, it is important that the ex-spouse not agree to a provision he or she does not intend to carry out. This sort of situation often reenacts the dynamics of the couple's dysfunctional marital relationship, in which a spouse caved in to the pressure of "I'm always right" but later tried to avoid complying. The parenting coordinator's strategy should be to encourage spouses to state their intentions honestly at coparenting sessions and to deal with the resulting disagreement in that environment. Noncompliance with an agreement in any form is likely to incense the "I'm always right" person and to put the children in the middle.

A second strategy for dealing with the "I'm always right"

parent involves taking away from him or her the power to make certain judgment calls. For example, Josh, an "I'm always right" father, frequently decided unilaterally that his boy was too sick to visit his mother. A clause had to be inserted in the agreement specifying that when the boy was ill, the custodial parent must take him to a doctor, who would certify that the child was too sick to be removed from the household. There may need to be several provisions of this sort to guard against the tendency of the "I'm always right" parent to coopt a disproportional amount of control.

Such people usually believe they have a special rapport with their children and insights no on else shares. They will insist on respecting children's needs and wishes but interpret them as consistent with their own. In a similar way, they will shape professional input and expertise to their own liking, or they will disregard it altogether, arguing that their knowledge of the children's best interests is superior to all others'. In some cases, this conviction grows until the parent comes to believe that no one else is worthy to teach values to or set behavioral standards for the children, especially the other parent. Children's constant exposure to such a model which empowers the child to this extent, may well lay the foundation of new "I'm always right" personalities.

A third strategy for successfully co-parenting with this defensive style is soliciting the input of the "I'm always right" parent into the initial agreement. The parent who has been active in formulating an agreement is far less likely to sabotage it later. One way to do this is to structure the first few co-parenting meetings as brainstorming sessions, in which the parents are encouraged to discuss many different suggestions. Then, when the final agreement is formulated, the coordinator can point out all the recommendations in it that originated with the "I'm always right" parent. Another way to pave the way for later compliance is to present several limited options to this parent and ask him or her either to elaborate on them or to choose one.

Finally, a strategy that limits the involvement of an ex-spouse's possible new relationship in co-parenting arrangements can prevent triggering the anger of the "I'm always right" parent. Indeed, parading this person in front of the latter is like waving a red flag. People with this defensive style often cannot bear the thought that they have been replaced as a love object; many will experience an acute sense of loss and humiliation. The ex-spouse needs to recognize that, for example, having the new girlfriend or boyfriend pick up the children for the weekend is too potent a reminder of loss. The agreement should therefore include language specifying that only the parents or some neutral person may pick up and deliver the children.

"You (Ex-Spouse) Are Always Wrong." There are a number of strategies to avoid setting off the reactivity of people with the "You're always wrong" defensive style. One is to ensure that they will not get the impression that information is being withheld from them. Like Lori, the mother whose letter to her ex-husband opens Chapter 1, these parents often accuse the ex-spouse of keeping back knowledge they need to parent effectively. They may become convinced, for example, that they are not receiving relevant educational, financial, and medical information about the children. Parents like these should not have to rely on each other for information. Agreements need to specify that each parent is responsible for setting up his or her own channels of communication with the professionals and instructors working with the children—whether teachers, coaches, or medical professionals.

A second strategy, containing the spread of the conflict or limiting "tribal welfare," is very important with "You're always wrong" parents. As these people are prone to promulgate their disparaging view of the ex-spouse, it may occasionally be helpful to involve the new spouse or extended-family members of "You're always wrong" people in mediation or co-parenting sessions. Doing so brings potential members of the tribal network into the structure of co-parenting, where their influence can be more easily channelled. In some cases, it may even be effective to include a special provision in the co-parenting agreement that gives helpful members of the external social-support network the opportunity to participate in co-parenting meetings on a limited basis and to share in responsibility for the children outside the sessions.

Another strategy useful to the ex-spouse of a "You're always wrong" is taking extra care not to demean him or her in public. Such people are especially vulnerable to public humiliation, even though they are all too likely to use this practice themselves. Even when the ex-spouse is feeling victimized and casting back blame can be very tempting, it solves nothing. If the "You're always wrong" person reinvents history and spreads distorted information to someone else, the other parent should deal directly with the other person as she or he would with a child in a loyalty bond, letting that person know that although another side to that story exists, she or he will not burden the other person with it or ask him or her to take sides. The opposite tactic, direct retaliation in kind, will only escalate conflict, provoking denials, self-justification, and a spiral of new accusations and externalizations.

Using the courtroom as a forum of public humiliation may "win battles but lose wars." When "You're always wrongs" lose, they often starts new litigation, find their own experts, and disparage those professionals who have offered opposing opinions in court. Public humiliation is likely to result in a renewed series of attacks on the ex-spouse.

There are, of course, times when the court must be utilized to enforce or define aspects of the co-parenting agreement. When this becomes necessary, the parenting coordinator should prepare the targeted parent to expect derogatory representations and a distorted picture of the situation. He or she will need to understand that these distortions are probably unavoidable and that responding in kind will only escalate the conflict. A therapist may be a helpful ally in finding strategies for sidestepping the effects of these direct onslaughts. With the exception of a few helpful others, it is best not to involve members of an external social network in the conflict when establishing the legal parameters of co-parenting with a "You're always wrong" person.

It is often a red flag to attempt to persuade "You're always wrong" individuals in intellectual argument by, for example, citing expert opinion or research findings. If they hold a fixed belief about something they will not be talked out of it by the presentation of new information; the tactic is far more likely to trigger anger. Alternatively, some of these people may reinterpret such data to support their own position. Others will enjoy using intellectual arguments as distracting games, reengaging the ex-spouse in arguing and redirecting discussion into unproductive channels. By the same token, it is not fruitful to try to dissuade ex-spouses from fixed negative beliefs about each other. The more effective strategy for the parenting coordinator is to refocus the discussion, bringing it back to the specifics of the children.

"Maybe I Will and Maybe I Won't." "Maybe I will and maybe I won't" people function happily in the midst of chaos and unpredictability. They interpret rules according to their own whims and behave in ways that constantly disappoint others' expectations. They derive a sense of safety and control from operating in this way. A strategy of simultaneously establishing clear expectations and anticipating unpredictable behavior can be written into co-parenting rules. It may be helpful, for example, to provide certain "socially acceptable outs" for not adhering to the agreement. Rather than setting up firm expectations, the agreement might provide for contingencies and the circumstances under which they may occur. It might, for example, state that "Visits will take place on Tuesday night if the parent can get free from work and has the money to put gas in the car. If not, they will not take place." Stating his or her intentions in this somewhat paradoxical form may enable this type of parent to follow through on them by creating a sense of not having been pinned down. This strategy also protects the children, who will learn not to expect predictable behavior from an unpredictable parent. If over time, however, the child's expectations are continually disappointed and the child is hurt by it, the provision must be revised to be more protective. One way to develop a sense of control in a situation that seems unpredictable is to be able to anticipate the behavior of the other person.

Especially in the early stages, an overall strategy of accepting partial and conditional agreements may be necessary with "Maybe I will and maybe I won't" people. For them, compliance with expectations means too much adherence to the control of others and a potential loss of identity. In negotiating agreements with this group, it is best to discuss topics one by one and to pin them down in stages. A conditional tone may be set by the parenting coordinator; he or she can express doubt about the workability of certain provisions, giving tacit permission to these people to react negatively. For example, the coordinator might say, "That might be a good idea, but we'll see if it really works." Stating expectations with some such degree of uncertainty may make such a person feel safer about actually satisfying them than if they were couched as absolute requirements.

An important strategy for helping "Maybe I will and maybe I won't" people carry out prior agreements is a commitment to writing down immediately any issue that is resolved. When a decision is not pinned down, these people are likely to want to "undo" and "redo" it, claiming that it is somehow unworkable. Establishing a clear schedule for reviewing specific parts of the agreement at specific intervals can help prevent such endless recapitulations of issues already settled. In the meantime, whenever possible, the agenda for sessions that are hammering out the co-parenting plan should be limited to new issues.

A sense of chaos may be present in these sessions. One strategy for containing confusion at this initial stage is to have two parenting coordinators. One can be a process facilitator, while the other remains focused on the agenda. The roles of the coordinators can switch back and forth; as one gets drawn into side issues with these chaos-prone clients, the other can pull the meeting back to the issue at hand.

Many "Maybe I will and and maybe I won't" parents will object to devising seemingly cumbersome rules for interaction and exchange. The very people who most need these rules and the external structure they impose are likely to ask, "Why can't we just be civil and reasonable with each other?" The meetings will give the parenting coordinator opportunities to emphasize that the structured interactions are stepping-stones—and incentives—leading to future "normal" co-parenting. He or she will make it clear that achieving success in reducing conflict will permit a relaxation of regulation and the creation of an atmosphere of openness and cooperation.

Easy-to-Victimize Ex-Spouses. Easy-to-victimize ex-spouses are highly vulnerable to hopes of reconciliation. At least during initial stages of co-parenting, holding separate sessions with each parent may help control this tendency. A mind set that reframes the former marital relationship as a business relationship centered on parenting the children will also help them redefine themselves as separate individuals.

Easy-to-victimize people often remain vulnerable to the disapproval of the ex-spouse, who can still produce feelings of uneasiness and guilt. They may perpetuate the conflict in their own minds by replaying the self-destructive putdowns of the ex-spouse or, even of their own hypercritical parents during childhood. They are likely to invite others to confirm their self-criticisms. Such parents often find that groups and/or individual therapy can help them build a new supportive social network to replace a censorious ex-spouse. Identifying the tendency toward negative "self-talk" and recommending books or classes that teach them how to send positive messages to themselves may also be a worthwhile strategy.

One of the frequent triggers of conflict between a highly dependent ex-spouse and one of the three conflict initiator types is the process of joint decision making. The parenting coordinator's presence as a mediator will usually assist in this process and enable easy-to-victimize people to build self-confidence. Similarly, when his or her strivings toward independence trigger conflict with an "I'm always right" individual resentful of the formerly dependent ex-spouse's newfound strength, the coordinator's strategy will be to support the growth.

Behavioral Modifications and Practical Suggestions for Interactional Impasse

High-conflict couples most frequently fight about the details of visitation, parenting approaches, and the exchange of information about their children. Modifying the way these elements of co-parenting are carried out can often minimize the children's exposure to conflict. The following sections discuss several strategies that may be useful. The details of the strategies to be adopted should be specified in the family's co-parenting plan.

Delivery, Not Pickup. If both parents can drive, a strategy of delivering the children to each other's homes rather than picking them up should be used. With high-conflict parents a familiar scenario is often acted out when, for example, the mother arrives to pick up the child at the father's home. The child is not yet ready, and as the mother waits impatiently in the doorway, the child and the father begin to say good-bye. The father feels that he is being rushed and perhaps deprived of some of his time with the child, or that his privacy has been invaded. The situation is generally tense and can easily erupt into open conflict.

A more relaxed transition could be achieved by arranging to say good-bye privately in the father's home. Then he and the child can pack up the latter's belongings and drive to the mother's house. A psychological message is inherent in such a procedure. The father is saying, in effect, "I'm delivering you to your mother and approve of your visit to her. Have a safe and enjoyable stay. We've said our good-byes. I'll be fine while you're gone and look forward to seeing you when you return."

Written Log. It is extremely helpful to have a written log, perhaps a small spiral notebook, that travels with the child, especially a very young one. It can contain information about preferred or disliked foods, medications, naps, scheduled activities, and so on. It is a useful way to exchange information between parents who are likely to trade angry words during the children's transitions. If the log is used to send messages of hostility and criticism, however, the coordinator will need to define how to use it more appropriately.

Neutral Drop-Off. A neutral drop-off point may become necessary if parents cannot contain their ire during transitions. This is especially important with young children, who cannot get from the car to the house or apartment on their own. Sometimes professionals or trusted friends or relatives are willing to have the children dropped off at their home or office, or they may undertake to drive the children to the parent's household. If conflict remains high, however, it may be necessary to reconfigure the visitation plan, decreasing the number of transitions necessary by substituting a longer visit for several short ones. While this procedure may run somewhat contrary to young children's developmental needs, it is best to give priority to minimizing their exposure to parental conflict and keeping them out of the middle. The parenting coordinator will generally consider the neutral drop-off an interim measure and will encourage parents to work toward normal transitions by reducing conflict.

Scheduling for neutral drop-offs should be done as far in advance as possible, preferably on a regular weekly basis. It will help the person who is facilitating the exchange to know, for example, that the child will be dropped off every Friday afternoon or that he or she will be picking up the child at one parent's house every Monday morning. Last-minute changes cause too much confusion when an additional person is involved.

Public Drop-Off. A less drastic measure than the neutral drop-off is the use of some public point for exchanging the children. A public library or museum accessible to both parents may provide a stimulating environment for the child while waiting. Parents have also been known to utilize shopping malls, restaurants, and hotel lobbies. Any public space will usually suffice to keep the parents on their most formal behavior toward each other. The most extreme sample we know is the couple who could contain their mutual animosity only by exchanging their children at the local police station.

Schedule Changes. Insofar as possible, all exceptions to the basic visitation schedule should be delineated in detail in writing. For example, descriptions of the terms of holiday visits should specify exact times; a given holiday, for example, may be defined as running from 9 A.M. one day to 9 A.M. the next day. Although neither parents nor coordinator will be able to anticipate all situations, being as specific as possible will help prevent renewal of conflict.

Special Events. When parents are unable to celebrate special events peaceably in each other's presence, it is best to hold celebrations in both houses. Children are not at all likely to object, for example, to celebrating their birthdays twice, once in each household. So instead of specifying who gets the child's birthday each year, it can be celebrated according to the calendar, wherever he or she would normally spend that day. For Christmas or Hannukah, children can either alternate between households from year to year or spend part of the holiday at each home, perhaps spending Christmas Eve through 10 A.M. Christmas Day at Mom's house and the rest of the day at Dad's. This sort of time schedule can be alternated from year to year as well.

Some events, however, cannot be duplicated or divided. In the case of children's recitals or special school programs, parents should agree to keep away from each other if there is a chance they will argue. All too often, we hear children talk about looking forward to performing in the school play but fearing that their parents will spoil the occasion by fighting in front of their friends and teachers. Parents who cannot maintain some physical distance from each other at school events should agree to divide them, even though this means missing some of the milestone events of their children's lives. During the regular season, it will be easy enough to alternate attendance at games or athletic matches; play-off and championship matches, however, pose a harder challenge, especially as the children probably will want both parents to attend. Here again, if they cannot do so without conflict, they will need to divide up these events as well.

Sharing Possessions. It is likely to cause less dissension if children move between households with as little baggage as possible. Keeping a complete set of clothes at each parent's house, with the exception of such expensive items as winter coats, is best if it is financially feasible. Costly items such as skis, bicycles, and computers may have to be sent back and forth when needed but should return to the home of the parent who purchased them or who maintains them. If equipment is damaged, responsibility for repair or replacement will lie with the parent with whom the child was resident when the damage occurred. As a general principle, it is well to keep in mind that sharing possessions between households increases the likelihood of disruptive arguments between parents.

Telephone Access. Ordinarily children should be allowed to telephone each parent from the other's home and should be assured of privacy during these calls. Sometimes, however, numerous nonemergency calls to or from the other parent constitute an annoyance and are disruptive to the visit. When this occurs, the time and frequency of telephone calls need to be limited so as not to intrude on family life. They should not, for example, be made at mealtime or homework time or after the child's bedtime.

Irregular Schedules. Visiting problems sometimes arise because of parents who do irregular shift work or travel a great deal on business. In these cases, the parenting agreement should provide several optional "mommy days" or "daddy days" each month to use in case of unavoidable scheduling changes. Obviously, these additional days should be scheduled as far in advance as possible so as to avoid disrupting the other parent's schedule.

Makeup Time. The parenting plan will specify that parents should not expect to receive makeup time for missed visits. When a parent needs to request a change in the schedule, he or she will go through the parenting coordinator or, if the parents have made progress in dealing directly with each other, will present the request to the other parent in written or spoken form. A parent who is unable to provide care during a scheduled period—at least a four-hour block—must give the other parent the first right of refusal to provide child care. If the latter cannot be available, the scheduled parent remains responsible for making other arrangements. When making a trade-off, a parent may request makeup time, but the other parent is not required to accommodate him or her. Parents should not demand or expect lengthy explanations for schedule modifications or for refusals or inabilities to accommodate to requested changes.

Introducing New Parenting Figures to Children. It occasionally happens that a child becomes attached to a parent's new significant other before the parent does. While a parent and his or her friend are still exploring the possibility of a serious relationship, the child may come to rely on the dating partner for support or a sense of an intact family. Parents, therefore, will need to agree that they will not bring a new person into their children's lives until there is some commitment to a long-term relationship. This judgment must, of course, be left to each parent; neither parent should be entitled to dictate the other parent's dating behavior.

When such new relationships are established, parents need to feel sure that their own importance to the children will not be diminished, no matter what the children call the new person. Some parents, for example, object to the child's calling a stepparent "Dad" or "Mom." It is probably best, however, to allow the child to use the name that feels most comfortable as long as he or she recognizes clearly that "Mom" will always be "Mom" and "Dad" will always be "Dad."

Supporting the Role of the Other Parent. During co-parenting sessions and in other interactions, the parenting coordinator will emphasize the benefits the child derives from his or her relationship with the other parent. Many parents need help in understanding how to support each other both verbally and behaviorally, for example, by delivering children to the other parent's home cheerfully and on time.

Limiting the Spread of Conflict

An external social network can be either a help or a hindrance to co-parenting. In general, the parenting coordinator should avoid seeking information from anyone but the parents, the children, and those professionals involved with the children or family members.

When not used to denigrate the other parent, a network can assist in the development of cooperative co-parenting. The network members may, for example, prove beneficial in an impasse situation in which derogatory beliefs about an ex-spouse are rigidly entrenched. A trusted relative or friend may have a more flexible outlook and may be able to soften the parent's attitude. Occasionally, a new spouse, a grandparent, or a supportive friend may play this role. Bringing him or her into several co-parenting sessions may help break through a difficult impasse. It is important to limit the involvement of those within the external-social network who have been destructive because of their participation in the negative reconstruction of the history of the relationship. If these individuals are unable to change their view, they will hinder the process of cooperative co-parenting.

The Children's Input

Throughout implementation of a co-parenting plan the parenting coordinator is likely to be subject to pressure by vocal, demanding, and persuasive parents. It is essential that he or she keep focused on the coordinator's primary mandate: to protect the children from conflict and to design strategies that will allow them to maintain ongoing, safe, peaceful relationships with both parents.

Occasional reevaluations of the children may be necessary to carry out this mandate. Even after initial assessments have been carried out and the co-parenting plan has been in operation for some time, the coordinator will retain the option to meet with and assess the children. Each coordinator will reach an individual decision about such interviews—based on his or her own knowledge of the children and on information about the parents' conflict or the children's behavior from a therapist or a recent custody evaluation. Some guidelines, however, are useful. Other than in situations of dangerousness, which present a special set of circumstances requiring a thorough outside assessment, children need to be evaluated whenever

- They show symptoms of distress.
- The parents disagree about their children's needs.
- The parents have widely varying descriptions of their children's behavior and its causes.
- The children ask to talk with the parenting coordinator.
- The children are firmly aligned with one parent.
- The children refuse to visit one parent.

In determining whether to interview the children, either together or as individuals, the parenting coordinator will need to be sensitive to the way children of different ages experience conflict. As discussed in detail in Chapter 3, their ages and the length of time they have been caught in interparental hostility determine children's long-term adjustment to the changes brought about by divorce.

Sometimes the coordinator will decide to interview a child to clarify the parents' differing descriptions of the child's disturbed behavior or wish for a change. Frequently parents in conflict attribute any change in behavior or childish fear to the other parent's actions. For example, Kevin, a five-year-old boy, suddenly began to refuse overnight visits with his father. Although his parents, Mike and Susan, had been in moderate conflict since their divorce two years earlier, a carefully designed visitation plan had protected Kevin from the worst of the conflict. On Wednesday evenings Susan dropped him at his father's house, and Mike returned him to school on Thursday mornings. For almost a year Kevin had maintained this schedule quite happily. Now, Susan announced, she wanted Kevin to return to her by 8:00 P.M. instead of staying overnight with Mike. She asserted that his father had failed to decorate Kevin's room in his new townhouse attractively and was not engaging him in play or other enjoyable activities. She was sure the boy was not having fun on his visits.

Mike reluctantly acknowledged that Kevin had voiced some mild concerns, but he felt convinced the boy was just passing through a stage and that it would soon be over. He saw no reason to modify visitation. Mike reported that he and Kevin usually went to the indoor pool in his townhouse complex and had fun together. Kevin had pinned up his own drawings on the bedroom walls and was happy to be allowed to decorate his room in his own way.

Because the parents interpreted the situation in such different ways, the parenting coordinator decided to do her own brief assessment of Kevin's state of mind. (Had there been a therapist working with the boy, the information would have been more readily available.) When contacted, Kevin's teacher reported that he did seem somewhat distracted and unable to settle into the daily routine on Thursday mornings. She described this as a fairly recent pattern of behavior. She added that Kevin's mother was extremely concerned and had told her that Kevin's relationship with his father was deteriorating and that she was planning to suspend the overnights.

When the coordinator met with the boy, the problem surfaced quickly. Kevin was afraid of spiders and was convinced that lots of them lurked in his father's basement. He was afraid to fall asleep at night, certain that they would crawl up the stairs and into his room. He had not told his father of his fears as he did not want to hurt Mike's feelings about the new home he was so proud of. Although Kevin had requested Mike to close the basement door, Mike sometimes forgot.

Compared to many encountered in high-conflict families, this was a simple problem with a simple solution. Kevin was trying bravely to master his fears on his own. Like many children of this age—almost six—he wanted to please his father and keep their relationship strong. His mother, always watchful for signs of poor parenting on her ex-husband's part, sensed that something was amiss. Rather than seeking out the underlying cause, she had jumped to a conclusion that fit her biased view of Mike: that he was failing to build a good relationship with their son.

What might have escalated into denied visitation and another court hearing was solved easily by closing the basement door. Susan stewed for a short time, annoyed that the assessment had failed to uncover evidence of Mike's shortcomings. Mike, on the other hand, needed to be helped to see that reminding his ex-wife of her mistake would only provoke tension and harm the boy. Kevin settled back into his relationship with his father and was sleeping well soon after the basement door was shut.

Parents like Kevin's are likely to use their children's difficulties in adjusting to new situations and their short-term developmental problems as confirmation of their own well-entrenched suspicions. In this case, as in others, the parenting coordinator was able to prevent an age-appropriate reaction to something unrelated to parenting from triggering another round of old issues and renewed animosity.

Appendix A
Parenting Plan

Stipulations Regarding Parenting

1. As stipulated in the final divorce decree, the Petitioner ("mother") shall have sole legal and physical custody of the two minor children, Michael, age four, and David, age eighteen months.

2. Both parties have agreed to use the services of (*insert name*) as a parenting coordinator to determine the best interests of the children as well as to mediate any disputes that may arise. Initially, appointments will be scheduled no less than every ninety days to discuss the parenting plan. These appointments may taper to a less frequent schedule, or to an as-needed basis, only with the agreement of both parties.

3. The primary residence of the children shall be with the mother. The children will visit with their father according to the following schedule:

Michael and David shall both be picked up by their father at 5:30 P.M. on Saturday evenings. David will be returned to his mother's home by 7:30 P.M. the same Saturday evening. Michael will spend Saturday evening at his father's home and will be returned to his mother's residence by 6:30 P.M. on Sunday evening.

In addition, Michael will be picked up by his father on Tuesday evenings at 5:30 P.M. and returned to his mother's home no later than 8:00 P.M. the same evening. On the evenings when Michael has a swimming lesson, his mother will feed him dinner prior to his pickup time of 5:30 P.M.

David will visit alone with his father on Thursday evenings from 5:30 P.M. until 7:30 P.M.

All pickup times by the father will be within thirty minutes of the times specified.

4. At such time as the mother finds full-time employment, the above-noted visitation schedule will be modified to equalize each parent's weekend time with the children while still preserving what is within the children's developmental needs. Revisions of the visitation schedule will be accomplished through joint meetings held with the parenting coordinator.

5. If the above-noted visitation schedule cannot be adhered to, the father will notify the mother with four days' notice of any change in the pickup time. Provided the father can arrive within thirty minutes of his pickup time, his visitation time will be honored. If the father cannot arrive within thirty minutes, his visitation will be forfeited if it is a Tuesday or Thursday evening. If the father cannot arrive within thirty minutes of his Saturday pickup time, visitation will not be forfeited, but it will be postponed and will begin at 8:00 A.M. on Sunday morning. If the mother finds it necessary to hire a babysitter between the hours of the father's visitation, even when notified of a late arrival, then the expense of these sitting arrangements will be borne by father since this time period covers his usual and customary visitation.

6. Mother and father agree to confer annually about this visitation schedule. As the children grow older and their developmental needs change, both parties agree to work together or with the assistance of the parenting coordinator to modify the visitation schedule to take into account these changing needs.

7. Both parties have agreed that church attendance is desirable for the children. Of the four weekends each month, church attendance will occur according to the following schedule: two

weekends per month, the mother will pick up the children from the father's residence to attend church from 8:30 A.M. until 10:15 A.M. on Sunday. She will return the children to the father's residence to continue their weekend visitation following church. Two weekends per month, the father will be responsible for church attendance for the children.

8. The parties agree that they will share holiday visitation with the children according to the following schedule: Christmas Eve and Christmas Day of 1989 will be spent with the mother as agreed upon in the temporary order of February 7, 1989. Commencing in January 1990, the father shall have the children on New Year's Eve (1989) and New Year's Day (1990) and on Christmas Eve and Christmas Day in December 1990. The mother shall have the children on the day prior to Easter and Easter Day in 1990 and on Thanksgiving Day in 1990. The schedule shall then rotate, with the father having Christmas Eve and Christmas Day in even-numbered years plus the following Easter. The mother shall have New Year's Eve and New Year's Day and the succeeding Thanksgiving of the year following a Christmas visit with the father. The order shall then reverse for the odd-numbered years, with the mother having Christmas Eve and Christmas Day and the following Easter. Christmas, New Year's, and Easter shall all be considered two-day holidays to commence at 8:00 A.M. on the eve of the holiday and to conclude at 9:00 P.M. the evening of the holiday. Thanksgiving shall be considered a one-day holiday to commence at 8:00 A.M. and conclude at 9:00 P.M.

Because the Christmas holidays are a very special time that both parents desire to spend with their children, each party agrees to be considerate of the feelings of the other and to remain amenable to a short (two- to three-hour) visitation period on either Christmas Eve or Christmas Day with the parent who is not scheduled for that year's visitation, provided the children have remained within the Denver vicinity for their Christmas holiday.

9. Mother's Day shall be spent each year with the mother.

10. Father's Day shall be spent each year with the father.

11. Memorial Day, July Fourth, and Labor Day shall be determined by the Christmas visitation schedule according to the following arrangement. The parent who does not have Christmas and Easter visitation shall have Memorial Day and Labor Day. The parent who does have the Christmas and Easter visitation shall have July Fourth.

12. Holiday visitation shall take priority over all other regularly scheduled visitation.

13. Either party desiring to travel outside Colorado with the children must notify the other party, in writing, not less than two weeks prior to any travel. Travel will be allowed provided the children are gone no more than two days and phone contact with the other parent is maintained during the period the children are traveling. As David reaches age three, longer travel periods will be introduced.

14. Neither party shall move on a permanent basis from the five-county Metropolitan Denver area except upon written agreement from the other party or upon court order.

15. All prescription medication will be given at the times indicated by the physician's orders.

16. Michael will be put to bed at a reasonable hour on Saturday evenings so he will be awake for church attendance on Sunday morning.

17. The mother will not call the father at work, where he is unable to talk in private.

18. Recognizing that preschool attendance is an important primary educational experience for their children, the parties agree that Michael will attend preschool from the present until he enters kindergarten. Preschool will be provided for David from his third birthday until he enters kindergarten.

The selection of a preschool for the children shall be a jointly made decision according to the following procedure. The mother shall visit as many preschools as she wishes. When she has narrowed her choice to three, she shall notify the father as to the names and addresses of her three selections. The father shall then visit each one and rank-order his choices as number 1, 2, and 3. If the father's rank order concurs with the mother's then the first-ranked preschool shall be agreed upon. If, however, there is a disagreement between the two parties in the ranking of their choices, the final decision will be made in a joint meeting with the parenting coordinator.

Both parties agree to share the cost of preschool according to their respective proportion of the final financial arrangement.

19. Both parties agree that participation in extracurricular activities will become increasingly important as the children grow toward school age. Therefore, they have agreed to select one extracurricular activity for each child and to share the cost of this activity according to their respective proportion of the final financial arrangement. This activity is to be mutually agreed upon and based on the interests and skills of the child.

20. Both parties agree that financial planning to ensure their children the opportunity of a higher education is desirable. They have agreed to open a savings account in January 1991 for the sole benefit of the minor children. This account will be for the benefit of both children, to be divided equally when Michael, the older of the children, reaches college age. The account will require the signature of both parents for any withdrawal to be made, and bank statements will be sent to both parents on a regular basis. To ensure the growth of this account, both parties agree to deposit a sum of $40 per month commencing in January 1991.

21. Each year, both Michael and David will need to be provided with appropriate winter clothing, which is to include a parka, snow pants, and winter boots. The father shall purchase these items for Michael, and the mother shall purchase these items for David by September 1 prior to the winter season for which they will be needed. All other clothing for the children shall be the individual responsibility of each parent.

22. Toys will be shared between the two households in the following manner. Toys will be considered as belonging to the parent who either purchased them or received them as gifts. If the children wish to take toys out of the home to which they belong, they may do so with the exception of bicycles, videos, computer games, and anything considered expensive or fragile by the parent who purchased or received that item. If a toy has left the home to which it belongs, the party may request it back

by communicating with the other party in either verbal or written form. The party receiving such a request for the return of a toy must comply. Extensive moving of toys between the two households will be discouraged by the parents. However, the expressed wishes of the children will also be recognized and honored as possible. Any dispute as to the ownership of a previously purchased item or newly purchased item will be resolved only through a joint meeting with both parties present and the parenting coordinator.

23. Each parent will purchase a bed at his or her own expense for David when he is ready to move from his crib to an adult bed.

24. In order to allow the mother the occasional opportunity for a short weekend vacation with the children, she has the option of asking the father to give up his regularly scheduled Saturday evening visitation and to instead begin his visitation on Sunday morning at 9:30 A.M. The mother may exercise this option no more often than once in six-week period, and she must give one full week's notice of her intent to exercise this option.

Recommendations for the Benefit of the Children

1. Each parent agrees that when she or he has scheduled time with the children, she or he is totally responsible for the children during that time. This extends to "responsibility for the children's irresponsibility." Therefore, if the children have left items somewhere or need items that they don't have, the parent that they are staying with and scheduled to be with will be responsible for transporting the children to get these items, even if they are left with the other parent.

2. Both the mother and the father agree to make an effort not to be engaged in anger at the other parent in the presence of the children. Each parent will make an effort to deal with problems on his or her own and directly with the child without involving or accusing the other parent.

3. Both the mother and the father agree that not only is it best that the children to be left out of the middle of the conflict,

but it is also important that others not be involved. These include friends, extended family, and others involved with the children, such as sitters, teachers, and day-care providers.

4. Both parents will be available to the children during their designated time. It is extremely important that the father be available to the children, as his time with them is limited. It is recommended that the father will make all efforts to be attentive and to actively parent the children during the time they are with him. The father is encouraged not to ask others for help such as driving or sitting.

5. It would be very helpful if the mother would make statements to the children that she values their relationship with their father and that their father is an integral and important shaping force in their lives. She will encourage them to enjoy their visits and will work toward developing a sense of trust in the father's parenting style and approach. If Michael calls her when he is with his father, she will tell him he is "to work it out with his dad."

6. The father will make an effort to follow through on his promises and not to disappoint the children.

Appendix B
Parenting Checklist

In creating a parenting plan, the parenting coordinator is wise to be as specific as possible. Uncertainty fuels conflict for couples who are uncooperative. Each family situation is unique in the developmental needs of the children, the level of conflict, and the requirements for structure. The following checklist is to assist the coordinator in devising as clearly detailed a plan as possible. The checklist covers the main areas that typically need addressing for all families; the specifics within each area will vary from family to family.

Visitation Plan

Daily, weekly, or long-distance time share schedule
Drop off/pick up: where, time, how, who
Consideration of child's needs
Transportation between households: delivery or pick up
Penalty for late drop off or pick up
Rescheduling: canceled visits rescheduled?
Overnights: phasing in
Phasing in increased parental involvement
If visitation refusal is a problem, how will it be handled?
Responsibility for sick children

Trade off or Last Minute Changes

Is a right of refusal for babysitting to be accorded? A right of refusal means the other parent has first option for child care over and above a sitter for any length of time four hours or longer (a shorter length of time is an intrusion, a longer length of time is fine).

Must ask in writing or verbally, not via the children. The other parent responds yes or no with the understanding that no explanation is expected or sought.

Flexibility is a two-way process. For high-conflict parents, it is a good first step toward learning cooperative communication.

Phone Calls

Typically not regulated but if a problem, it needs to be

Typically, child can initiate phone calls in private at any time

Parent-initiated calls: if problematic, need to be scheduled; specify how long, how often and when or whether allowed

Toys and Belongings

Two complete sets are best.

Need guidelines for things moving between two households

Specify what travels and what cannot (example, expensive sports equipment)

Holiday Visitation

Holidays supersede regularly scheduled visitation with no make up expected. Christmas Eve, Christmas Day, New Year's Eve, New Year's Day, Spring Break, Easter, July 4th, Memorial Day, Labor Day, Halloween, Thanksgiving, Presidents Day, Passover, Rosh Hashanah, and other holidays of significance and/or time off from school.

Birthdays: children will celebrate two happily.
Father's Day and Mother's Day
Alternate arrangements:
    1. alternate odd/even years
    2. split holiday in mid-day
    3. Monday holidays must be specified whether attached to weekend visitation

Extracurricular Activities

If you expect the other parent to support your choice, then you must seek his or her endorsement.

Activities: who pays, provides transportation, and attends
Expensive equipment needs to be covered in financial
    agreement for clarity.

Religious Planning

Religious training and/or education
Frequency of church or synagogue attendance
Observing religious holidays
Other religious issues

Medical and Professional Appointments

Emergency: either parent can initiate
Regularly scheduled doctor's and dentist's appointments
An effort is made to keep other parent informed of prescriptions, illness, but ultimate responsibility rests with
    each parent to maintain communication with professionals working with the children
Evaluations for special needs
Communication with professionals
Ability to obtain records

Communication Plan

Need a plan for communication between the parents for moderate to severe conflict

Telephone permitted: when, where?
Appointments with coordinator
Notebook
Writing

School

Selection of school
Change of school
Access to teachers and conferences
Report cards
Back to school night
School events: attendance
Communication with school: responsibility of each parent
Projects of child—which parent helps

Vacations

Is out of state travel allowed?
Is out of country travel allowed?
How long: developmental considerations
Telephone contact with other parent
Sleeping arrangements while on vacation
Phone numbers left in case of emergency
Pre-planned vacations take precedence over regular visitation

Financial Planning for Future

College money
Special needs planning

Grandparents and Other Relatives

Extended family has access during child's regular visitation with that parent.

Typically not specified.

Endangerment

Each agrees other is safe or a provision for safety is inserted

Relatives, friends, and activities may need to be considered as well

Boundaries or Rules at Other Household

Basically neither parent may dictate to the other

If endangerment is an issue, parenting coordinator is to be contacted

Serious concerns about parental judgment are to be addressed to parenting coordinator

Is corporal punishment or other means of discipline an issue?

Including friends or pets on visits

Alternative Beliefs

If one parent objects to the other's belief systems, then boundaries and ground rules will need to be specified via the parenting coordinator

One parent cannot set the rules for the other's household

Significant Others and Dating

If relationship is truly seen as committed, then a gradual introduction of the significant other is suggested. Both parents need to clarify their values with the children.

Basically, one parent cannot dictate to the other his or her lifestyle.

Better to limit the children's involvement in relationships with others until long-term commitments are made.

Special Needs Considerations

Disability, physical or mental

Chronic medical conditions

Ethnic/cultural issues

Parenting Coordinator

Either parent has access to the parenting coordinator for dispute resolution at any time for any issue

Define emergency procedures for unexpected flare-ups of the conflict

Appendix C
Parenting Coordinator
Agreement

1. My role as parenting coordinator will be to assist both of you in resolving conflict in a manner that is beneficial to your child or children. You may have enlisted my services voluntarily or may have had such services stipulated by the court. Regardless, it is understood that I cannot change the legal custody status of the children. Major changes in the visitation schedule, as specified in your separation and/or divorce decree will not be made. The implementation of the visitation schedule, however, will be subject to my recommendations. The pacing of visitation, temporary changes in the schedule, and holiday or vacation planning will be addressed.

2. Whether appointments will be held jointly or individually will be at my discretion. Whether a situation requires an appointment or can be handled over the telephone will also be at my discretion.

3. Face-to-face appointments as well as telephone calls will be charged for at a rate of _____ per _____ minutes. In addition, all time involved in the preparation of written reports or communication with other professionals will be charged for at the same rate. Court time will be charged for,

including travel to and from court, at the rate of _____ per hour.

4. (Optional) There must be a retainer of $500 from each parent to initiate this parenting coordinator agreement. Money will be drawn from this retainer. The amount charged to each of you will be equally divided unless I am provided with a certified copy of your divorce decree stating clearly the manner in which medical expenses are to be divided between you. Upon receipt of such decree and with written authorization from both of you of such a stipulation, the retainer account will be charged according to your agreement regarding medical expenses.

[For Couples in Minimal, Mild, or Moderate Conflict]

5A. Conflict resolution or mediation is not a crisis service. The goal is for both of you to learn strategies for problem solving and conflict reduction. The expectation is that you will employ these strategies in solving the conflict and will delay the impulsive expression of anger. Therefore, I will expect both of you to schedule appointments by telephone in advance. Appointments will be held during regular business hours.

[For Couples in Moderately Severe or Severe Conflict]

5B. Conflict resolution or mediation is not a crisis service. Regular appointments will be scheduled and held during my business hours. I do recognize that a crisis situation might occur between our regularly scheduled appointments. A crisis is any situation that either of you feels endangers your child or children emotionally or physically. I will be available as possible for such emergency situations.

6. Throughout the course of serving as parenting coordinator, regular summary reports will be issued describing the nature of the conflict discussed and the recommended resolution. Copies of all reports will be sent to both of you (optional) as well as to each of your respective attorneys. Copies may be forwarded to the court at my discretion. Since written reports will be issued, it is understood that this is not a confidential process.

7. All therapists involved, attorneys involved, and previous or current evaluators are authorized to release information directly to me.

8. Financial matters will not be addressed as part of the parenting coordination.

[For All Parents with the Exception of Alienation]

9A. The coordinator reserves the right to withdraw from that role should he or she feel that effective mediation is no longer occurring. The parents as well as their respective attorneys will be given two weeks notice of the decision to withdraw. All money remaining in each retainer account will be refunded to the proper party. The names of three professionals competent to assume the role of coordinator will be provided to both parents.

[For Parental Alienation]

9B. Upon signing this agreement, it is understood that my services as a parenting coordinator cannot be terminated by either parent for a period of ———————— (specify one or two) year(s). Should I need to withdraw from my role as coordinator, notice will be given to both of you as well as to your respective attorneys. I will provide each of you with the names of three professionals competent to assume the role of parenting coordinator, and I will continue to act in that position until such time as a smooth transition has been achieved to the new coordinator. All money remaining in each retainer account will be refunded to the proper party.

Please sign below to indicate your understanding of this agreement. Upon receipt of a signed agreement from both parents as well as the $500 retainer fee, the parenting coordination process can proceed.

Date———————— Signature————————————

Date———————— Signature————————————

Appendix D
Child Therapist Agreement

1. My role as therapist for your child is to create a therapeutic and safe environment for the sharing of feelings related to your divorce. It is understood that my neutrality in any post-divorce disputes is for the benefit of your child.

2. Conflictual issues will not be addressed to me, as your child's therapist. Any concerns regarding visitation or parenting will be presented to the parenting coordinator.

3. It is understood that once therapy has commenced, I will share all information regarding the progress of therapy with the parenting coordinator and limit direct feedback to parents.

4. It is also understood that once therapy has commenced, I will not speak with either of your attorneys, nor will I appear in court proceedings related to divorce or visitation disputes. Any information necessary for such proceedings will be communicated by the parenting coordinator.

5. By signing this agreement, you give permission for me to release any and all information regarding the treatment of your child to the agreed-upon parenting coordinator. No information will be released at any time to any other individual without your specific consent.

6. Therapy will terminate at such time as the parenting coordinator and I agree that the goals of treatment have been accomplished.

7. In support of your child's therapy, each of you, by signing this agreement, acknowledges your willingness to cooperate by providing transportation to and from the therapy hour at the agreed-upon day and time.

_____   _____

(Signature of father)   (Date)

_____   _____

(Signature of mother)   (Date)

References

Chapter 1

1. Eleanor Maccoby and Robert Mnookin. (1992). *Dividing the Child*. Cambridge: Harvard University Press.

Chapter 2

1. J. Wallerstein. (1991). The long term effects of divorce on children: A review. *Journal of American Academy of Child Psychiatry*, 30(3):349–360.
2. S. Silvestri, (1991) Marital instability in men from intact and divorced families: Interpersonal, behavior, cognitions and intimacy. Paper presented at The American Psychological Association Convention, San Francisco.
3. J. Wallerstein. (1983). Children of divorce: The psychological tasks of the child. *American Journal of Orthopsychiatry*, 53:263–279.
4. S. Chess and A. Thomas. (1986). *Temperament in Clinical Practice*. New York: Guilford Press.
5. J. Guidubaldi and J. D. Perry. (1985). Divorce and mental health sequelae for children: A two year follow up of a nationwide sample. *Journal of American Academy of Child Psychiatry*, 24:531–537.
6. Joan Kelly and Judith Wallerstein. (1980). Crisis in the classroom. *Working Mother* (March) pp. 41–93.
7. J. Wallerstein and S. Blakeslee. (1989). *Second Chances*. New York: Ticknor & Fields.
8. E. M. Hetherington, S. Hagan, and E. R. Anderson. (1989). Marital transitions: A child's perspective. *The American Psychologist*, 44(2):303–312.
9. L. J. Weitzman. (1985). *The Divorce Revolution: The Unexpected Social and Economic Consequences for Women and Children in America*. New York: Free Press.

173

10. A. L. Stolberg, C. Camplair, K. Currier, and M. J. Wells. (1987). Individual, familial, and environmental determinants of children's post divorce adjustment and maladjustment. *Journal of Divorce,* 11:51–70.

11. J. Santrock and R. Warshak. (1979). Father custody and social development in boys and girls. *Journal of Social Issues,* 35:112–125.

12. K. Camera and G. Resnick. (1988). Interparental conflict and cooperation: Factors moderating children's post divorce adjustment. In E. M. Hetherington and J. D. Arasteh (Eds.), *Impact of Divorce, Single Parenting and Stepparenting on Children* (pp. 169–195). Hillsdale, N.J.:Erlbaum.

13. F. Furstenberg and C. Nord. (1985). Parenting apart: Patterns of childrearing after marital disruption. *Journal of Marriage and the Family,* 47:843–904.

14. Eleanor Maccoby and Robert Mnookin. (1992). *Dividing the Child.* Cambridge: Harvard University Press.

15. J. Johnston, L. Campbell, and M. Tall. (1985). Impasses to the resolution of custody and visitation disputes. *American Journal of Orthopsychiatry,* 55:112–129.

16. M. Baris and C. Garrity. (1988). *Children of Divorce: A Developmental Approach to Residence and Visitation.* DeKalb, Ill.: Psy Tec.

17. William Hodges. (1986). *Interventions for Children of Divorce.* New York: Wiley.

18. Neil Kalter. (1990). *Growing Up with Divorce.* New York: Free Press.

19. D. R. Coller. (1988). Joint custody: Research, theory, and policy. *Family Process,* 27:459–469.

20. P. D. Allison and F. F. Furstenberg, Jr. (1989). How marital dissolution affects children. *Developmental Psychology,* 25:540–549.

21. I. N. Sandler, S. A. Wolchik, and S. L. Braver. (1988). The stressors of children's postdivorce environments. In Sharlene Wolchik and Paul Karoly (Eds.), *Children of Divorce: Empirical Perspectives on Adjustment* (pp. 111–143). New York: Gardner Press.

Chapter 3

1. J. Johnston and L. Campbell. (1988). *Impasses of Divorce.* New York: Free Press.

2. J. Wallerstein. (1991). The long term effects of divorce on children: A review. *Journal of American Academy of Child Psychiatry,* 30(3):349–360.

3. Robert Mnookin. (1992). Dividing the child: How professionals can help parents make decisions. Paper presented at 16th Annual Child Custody Conference, Keystone, Colo.

4. S. Silvestri. (1991). Marital instability in men from intact and divorced families: Interpersonal behavior, cognitions and intimacy. Paper presented at the American Psychological Association Convention, San Francisco, Calif.

5. Hara Marano. (1992). Reinvention of marriage. *Psychology Today* (January–February), pp. 48–53.

6. E. M. Hetherington. (1989). Coping with family transitions: Winners, losers and survivors. *Child Development,* 60:1–14.

7. R. Felner, L. Terra, and R. Rowlinson. (1988). A life transition framework for understanding marital dissolution and family reorganization. In Sharlene Wolchik and Paul Karoly (Eds.), *Children of Divorce: Empirical Perspectives on Adjustment* (pp. 35–65). New York: Gardner Press.
8. J. Wallerstein and S. Blakeslee. (1989). *Second Chances*. New York: Ticknor & Fields.
9. A. Cherlin, F. Furstenberg, Jr., C. Lansdale, P. Lindsay, K. Keirnan, P. Robins, D. Morrison, and J. Teitler. (1991). Longitudinal studies of effects of divorce on children in Great Britain and the United States. *Science*, 252:1386–1388.

Chapter 4

1. J. Fantuzzo, L. DePaola, L. Lambert, T. Martino, G. Anderson, and S. Sutton. (1991). Effects of interparental violence on the psychological adjustment and competencies of young children. *Journal of Consulting and Clinical Psychology*, 59(2):258–265.
2. E. M. Cummings, M. Ballard, M. El-Sherkh, and M. Lake. (1991). Resolution and children's responses to interadult anger. *Developmental Psychology* 27(3):462–470.
3. J. Wallerstein and S. Corbin. The child and the vicissitudes of divorce. In Melvin Lewis (Ed.), (1991) *Child and Adolescent Psychiatry* (pp. 1108–1118). Baltimore: Williams & Wilkins.
4. J. Kelly. (1987). Longer-term adjustment in children of divorce: Converging findings and implications for practice. Paper presented at the Annual Meeting of the American Psychological Association, New York.
5. K. Camera and G. Resnick. (1988). Interparental conflict and cooperation: Factors moderating children's post divorce adjustment. In E. M. Hetherington and J. D. Arasteh (Eds.), *Impact of Divorce, Single Parenting and Stepparenting on Children* (pp. 169–195). Hillsdale, N.J.: Erlbaum.
6. Robert Mnookin. (1992). Dividing the child: How professionals can help parents make decisions. Paper presented at 16th Annual Child Custody Conference, Keystone, Colorado.
7. M. Baris and C. Garrity. (1988). *Children of Divorce: A Developmental Approach to Residence and Visitation*. DeKalb, Ill.: Psy Tec.
8. S. Friedman. (1988). A family systems approach to treatment. In Lenore Walker (Ed.), *Handbook on Sexual Abuse of Children* (pp. 326–349) New York: Springer.

Chapter 5

1. R. Felner, L. Terra, and R. Rowlinson. (1988). A life transition framework for understanding marital dissolution and family reorganization. In Sharlene Wolchik and Paul Karoly (Eds.), *Children of Divorce: Empirical Perspectives on Adjustment* (pp. 35–65). New York: Gardner Press.
2. William Hodges. (1986). *Interventions for Children of Divorce*. New York: Wiley.

3. W. G. Clingempeel, M. S. Shwall, and E. Heiss. (1988). Divorce and remarriage: Perspectives on the effects of custody arrangements on children. In Sharlene Wolchik and Paul Karoly (Eds.), *Children of Divorce: Empirical Perspectives on Adjustment* (pp. 145–181). New York: Gardner Press.
4. J. Johnston and L. Campbell. (1988). *Impasses of Divorce.* New York: Free Press.
5. M. Baris and C. Garrity. (1988). *Children of Divorce: A Developmental Approach to Residence and Visitation.* DeKalb, Ill.: Psy Tec.
6. J. Wallerstein and S. Blakeslee. (1989). *Second Chances.* New York: Ticknor & Fields.
7. R. E. Emery. (1989). Family violence. *American Psychologist,* 44:321–328.
8. Male victims of domestic violence still in the closet. (1992). *Rocky Mountain News* (July 13).
9. S. Friedman. (1988). A family systems approach to treatment. In Lenore Walker (Ed.), *Handbook on Sexual Abuse of Children* (pp. 326–349) New York: Springer.

Chapter 6

1. R. Gardner. (1986). *Child Custody Litigation.* Creskill, N.J.: Creative Therapeutics.
2. Association of Family and Conciliation Courts. (1988). *The Sexual Abuse Allegation Project: Final Report.* AFCC, 1720 Emerson St., Denver, Colo. 80218.
3. Leona Kopetsky. (1991). Parental alienation syndrome: Recent research. Paper presented at 15th Annual Child Custody Conference, Keystone, Colo.
4. R. Gardner. (1981). *The Parental Alienation Syndrome and the Differentiation between Fabricated and Genuine Child Sex Abuse.* Creskill, N.J.: Creative Therapeutics.
5. R. Gardner. (1992). *The Parental Alienation Syndrome.* Creskill, N.J.: Creative Therapeutics.
6. J. Johnston. (1993). Children of divorce who refuse visitation. In Charlene Depner and James Bray (Eds.), *Non-Residential Parenting* (pp. 109–135). Newbury Park, Calif.: Sage Publications.
7. J. Wallerstein and S. Corbin. The child and the vicissitudes of divorce. In Melvin Lewis (Ed.), (1991) *Child and Adolescent Psychiatry* (pp. 1108–1118). Baltimore, Md.: Williams & Wilkins.
8. S. Clawar and B. Rivlin. (1991). *Children Held Hostage: Dealing with Programmed and Brainwashed Children.* Chicago, Illinois American Bar Association.
9. J. Johnston and L. Campbell. (1988). *Impasses of Divorce.* New York: Free Press.

Chapter 7

1. M. Baris and C. Garrity. (1988). Appendix in *Children of Divorce: A Developmental Approach to Residence and Visitation.* DeKalb, Ill.: Psy Tec.
2. George Newman. (1981). *101 Ways to Be a Long Distance Super-Dad.* Saratoga, Calif.: Blossom Valley Press.

Chapter 8

1. J. Johnston and L. Campbell. (1988). *Impasses of Divorce*. New York: The Free Press.
2. Eleanor Maccoby and Robert Mnookin. (1992). *Dividing the Child: Social and Legal Dilemmas of Custody*. Cambridge: Harvard University Press.

Chapter 9

1. J. Johnston and L. Campbell. (1988). *Impasses of Divorce*. New York: Free Press.

Bibliography

Allison, P. D., and Furstenberg, F. F., Jr. (1989) How marital dissolution affects children. *Developmental Psychology,* 25:540–549.

Association of Family and Conciliation Courts. (1988). *The Sexual Abuse Allegation Project: Final Report.* AFCC, 1720 Emerson St., Denver, Colo. 80218.

Baris, M., and Garrity, C. (1988). *Children of Divorce: A Developmental Approach to Residence and Visitation.* DeKalb, Ill.: Psy Tec.

Camera, K., and Resnick, G. (1988). Interparental conflict and cooperation: Factors moderating children's post divorce adjustment. In E. M. Hetherington & J. D. Arasteh (Eds.,) *Impact of Divorce, Single Parenting and Stepparenting on Children* (pp. 169–195). Hillsdale, N.J.: Erlbaum.

Chess, S., and Thomas A. (1986). *Temperament in Clinical Practice.* New York: Guilford Press.

Clawar, S., and Rivlin, B. (1991). *Children Held Hostage: Dealing with Programmed and Brainwashed Children.* Chicago, Illinois. American Bar Association.

Clingempeel, W. G., Shwall, M. S., and Heiss, E. (1988). Divorce and remarriage: Perspectives on the effects of custody arrangements on children. In Sharlene Wolchik and Paul Karoly (Eds.) *Children of Divorce: Empirical Perspectives on Adjustment* (pp. 145–181). New York: Gardner Press.

Coller, D. R. (1988). Joint custody: Research, theory, and policy. *Family Process,* 27:459–469.

Cummings, E. M., Ballard M., El-Sherkh, M., and Lake, M. (1991). Resolution and children's responses to interadult anger. *Developmental Psychology,* 27(3):462–470.

Emery, R. E. (1989). Family violence: *American Psychologist,* 44:321–328.

Fantuzzo, J., DePaola, L. Lambert, L., Martino, T., Anderson, G., and Sutton S. (1991). Effects of interparental violence on the psychological adjustment and competencies of young children. *Journal of Consulting and Clinical Psychology,* 59(2):258–265.

Felner, R., Terra, L., and Rowlinson, R. (1988). A life transition framework for understanding marital dissolution and family reorganization. In Sharlene Wolchik and Paul Karoly (Eds.), *Children of Divorce: Empirical Perspectives on Adjustment* (pp. 35–65). New York: Gardner Press.

Friedman, S. (1988). A family systems approach to treatment. In Lenore Walker (Ed.), *Handbook on Sexual Abuse of Children* (pp. 326–349). New York: Springer.

Gardner, R. (1986). *Child Custody Litigation.* Creskill, N.J.: Creative Therapeutics.

Guidubaldi, J., and Perry, J. D. (1985). Divorce and mental health sequelae for children: A two year follow up of a nationwide sample. *Journal of American Academy of Child Psychiatry,* 24:531–537.

Hetherington, E. M. (1980). Coping with family transitions: Winners, losers, and survivors. *Child Development,* 60:1–14.

Hetherington, E. M., Hagan, S., and Anderson, E. R. (1989). Marital transitions: A child's perspective. *The American Psychologist,* 44(2):303–312.

Hodges, William. (1986). *Interventions for Children of Divorce.* New York: Wiley.

Kalter, Neil. (1990). *Growing Up with Divorce.* New York: Free Press.

Kelly, J. (1987). Longer-term adjustment in children of divorce: Converging findings and implications for practice. Paper presented at the Annual Meeting of the American Psychological Association, New York.

Kopetsky, Leona. (1991). Parental alienation syndrome: Recent research. Paper presented at 15th Annual Child Custody Conference, Keystone, Colorado

Johnston, J., and Campbell, L. (1988). *Impasses of Divorce.* New York: Free Press.

Maccoby, Eleanor, & Mnookin, Robert. (1992). *Dividing the Child.* Cambridge: Harvard University Press.

Male victims of domestic violence still in the closet. (1992). *Rocky Mountain News* (July 13).

Marano, Hara. (1992). Reinvention of Marriage. *Psychology Today* (January–February), pp. 48–53.

Mnookin, Robert. (1992). Dividing the child: How professionals can help parents make decisions. Paper presented at 16th Annual Child Custody Conference, Keystone, Colo.

Newman, George. (1981). *101 Ways to Be a Long Distance Super-Dad.* Saratoga, Calif.: Blossom Valley Press.

Sandler, I. N., Wolchik, S. A., and Braver, S. L. (1988). The stressors of children's postdivorce environments. In Sharlene Wolchik and Paul Karoly (Eds.), *Children of Divorce: Empirical Perspectives on Adjustment* (pp. 111–143). New York: Gardner Press.

Santrock, J., and Warshak, R. (1979). Father custody and social development in boys and girls. *Journal of Social Issues,* 35:112–125.

Silvestri, S. (1991). Marital instability in men from intact and divorced families: Interpersonal behavior, cognitions and intimacy. Paper presented at the American Psychological Association Convention, San Francisco.

Stolberg, A. L., Camplair, C., Currier, K., and Wells, M. J. (1987). Individual, familial, and environmental determinants of children's post divorce adjustment and maladjustment. *Journal of Divorce,* 11:51–70.

Straus, M. A., Steinmetz, S. K., and Gelles, R. J. (1980). *Behind Closed Doors: Violence in the American Family.* Garden City, N.Y.: Anchor Books.

Wallerstein, J. (1991). The long term effects of divorce on children: A review. *Journal of American Academy of Child Psychiatry,* 30(3):349–360.

Wallerstein, J., and Blakeslee, S. (1989). *Second Chances.* New York: Ticknor & Fields

Wallerstein, J., & Corbin, S. The child and the vicissitudes of divorce. In Melvin Lewis (Ed.), (1991) *Child and Adolescent Psychiatry* (pp. 1108–1118). Baltimore: Williams & Wilkins.

Weitzman, L. J. (1985). *The Divorce Revolution: The Unexpected Social and Economic Consequences for Women and Children in America.* New York: Free Press.

Index

Abandonment, sudden, 105–6
Abuse
  child, 68
    evaluation of claims of, 68–69
    physical, 61
    sexual, 68
    spouse, 61–62
Academic performance, 15
Adjustment of children, 13–23
  age and, 14–15
  balancing factors in, 20–23
  contact with both parents and, 18
  environmental stability and, 16–17
  gender and, 15–16
  intensity of conflict between parents
    and, 19–20
  psychological functioning of resi-
    dential parent and, 17–18
  temperament and, 13–14
Adolescents, 15, 135–36
  coping with conflict by, 34
Age of child
  conflict levels and, 53–57
  coping with conflict and, 30–34
  postdivorce adjustment and, 14–15
  visitation schedule and, 85
Aggression, 19
Agreement
  Child Therapist, 88, 171–72
  Parenting, 136–37
  Parenting Coordinator, 168–70

Alienation. *See* Parental alienation
Ambivalent separation, 106
Anger
  easy-to-trigger, 115–18
  managing, 92
Arbitrator, parenting coordinator as,
  127
Assessment of conflict, 41–50
  Conflict Assessment Scale, 42–43,
    52
  mild conflict, 46–47
  minimal conflict, 45–46
  moderate conflict, 47–48
  moderately severe conflict, 48–49
  severe conflict, 49–50
  visitation and, 60–61, 63
Attorney, parental alienation and,
  80–81

Behavior modification, 146–50
Behavior problems, 19
Binds, loyalty, 24–26, 48, 88, 93,
  128, 129, 133, 136
Breakdown of marriage, sudden, 77

Campbell, Linda, 37, 62, 102, 103,
  104, 106, 134
Caretaking role, 39
"Caring-competent" class of children,
  39
Celebrations, 148

181

Checklist, parenting, 162–67
Child abuse, 68
  evaluation of claims of, 68–69
  physical, 61
  sexual, 68
Children of divorce. *See also* Adjust-
    ment of children; Adolescents;
    Development, effect of conflict
    on
  difficult, 14
  discussion of adult concerns with,
    79–80
  implementing decisions with,
    135–36
  interview by parenting coordinator
    of, 136, 151–54
  introducing new parenting figures
    to, 150
  lying by, 32
  as message bearers, 91
  psychological tasks facing, 12–13
  reaction to divorce, 11–12
  refusal of visitation by, 67–68,
    95–99
  resilient, 14
  side-taking by, 32, 33–34
  stress on, issues causing greatest, 26
  telephone access for, 149
  therapy for, 86–90
  well-adjusted, 13–20
Children of Divorce (Garrity &
    Baris), 52
Child Therapist Agreement, 88,
    171–72
Cognitive strategies for impasse inter-
    vention, 133–38
Communication, guidelines for par-
    ents, 137–38
"Competent" class of children, 39
Conflict(s). *See also* Assessment of
    conflict; Impasse
  children's methods of dealing with,
    37–40
  intensity of, 19–20
  limiting spread of, 151
  long-term outcome of, 26–28
  reasons for harmfulness of, 34–40
  subjects of, 23–26
Conflict Assessment Scale, 42–43, 52
Conflict levels, 52–64

  mild, 46–47, 52, 127–28
  minimal, 45–46, 52, 127–28
  moderate, 47–48, 52–59, 128, 129
  moderately severe, 48–49, 60–62,
    129–31
  severe, 49–50, 62–64, 129–31
Controlling personalities, 116–17
Cooperative co-parenting, 7–8, 18.
    See also Parenting plan
  construction of, 28
Coordinator, parenting. *See* Parenting
    coordinator
Coping methods, 37–40. *See also* De-
    fensive styles
Court system, 8. *See also* Litigation
Custody, 22–23
  joint, 22–23, 58
  switching of, 70
Custody evaluator, 120

Decisions, implementation with chil-
    dren, 135–36
Defenses, externalizing, 72
Defensiveness, potential triggers for,
    123
Defensive styles
  "easy-to-victimize ex-spouse," 118–
    19, 124
  "I'm always right," 111–13, 123,
    139–41
  "Maybe I will and maybe I won't,"
    115–18, 123–24
  parenting coordinator's knowledge
    of, 123–24
  "You're always wrong," 114–15,
    123, 141–43
Demarcated joint custody, 58
Denial, parental alienation and, 78
Depression, 19
Destructive legacy of marriage, 105
Devaluation, parental alienation and,
    78
Development, effect of conflict on
  age and, 30–34, 53–57
  parents as role models and, 35–36
  parents' role as children's protectors
    and, 35
  sidetaking and, 35
Development of coping methods and
    strategies, 37–40

Difficult children, 14
Diffusing, 38
Disengagement, emotional, 128–29
Disorder of the self, 106
Disparaging talk, 24
Dissonance, 89–90
Divorce decree, 51, 101
Drop-off points, 147

"Easy-to-victimize ex-spouse" defensive style, 118–19, 124, 145
Educational approach to cognitive and reframing strategies, 133
Eight-year olds, coping with conflict by, 31–33
Emotional outbursts, inciting, 80–81
Entitlement, sense of, 74
Environmental stability, children's postdivorce adjustment and, 16–17
Equilibrating, 37
Externalizing defenses, 72

Family dynamics, parental alienation and, 72–73
Family mediators, 8
Fathers, dropout rates of, 18
Fights, subjects of, 23–26. *See also* Conflict(s)
Financial concerns, discussing with children, 79–80
Five-year olds, coping with conflict by, 31
Four-year olds, coping with conflict by, 31

Geffner, Robert, 61
Gender of child, postdivorce adjustment and, 15–16
Guardians *ad litem*, 7

Hetherington, E. Mavis, 38–39
High-conflict parents, mediation for, 23

Identity
    denial of, 87–88
    formation of, 38
    lack of, 32–33
"I'm always right" defensive style, 111–13, 123, 139–41

Impasse, 102–19. *See also* Parenting plan
    external, social-network level of, 104–5
    high-risk types for, 111–19
        "easy-to-victimize ex-spouse," 118–19
        "I'm always right," 111–13
        "Maybe I will and maybe I won't," 115–18
        "You're always wrong," 114–15
    identifying triggers for, 139–45
    interactional level of, 105–6
    intrapsychic level of, 106–7
    levels of vulnerability and, 108–10
    model of, 103
Infidelity, parental alienation and, 75
Injuries, marital and divorce, 107–8
Input from children, utilizing, 136
Intervention for parental alienation. *See under* Parental alienation

Johnston, Janet, 37, 62, 102, 103, 104, 106, 132, 134
Joint custody, 22–23
    demarcated, 58

Legacy of truly destructive marriage, 105
Legal system, 8
Litigation
    parental alienation and, 80–81, 83
    tribal warfare and, 104
    "You're always wrong" types and, 142
Log for children, written, 146–47
Loyalty binds, 24–26, 48, 88, 93, 128, 129, 133, 136
Lying by children, 32

Makeup time, 149–50
Maneuvering, 37
Marital breakdown, sudden, 77
Marital violence, 61–62
"Maybe I will and maybe I won't" defensive style, 115–18, 123–24, 143–45
Mediation, 7, 63, 119–20
    for high-conflict parents, 23
Mediators, family, 8

Meetings, parenting, 133–34
Mental health professionals, 7, 63. *See also* Therapist(s)
  tribal warfare and, 104–5
Merging, 37–38
Messages, children as bearers of, 91
Mild conflict level, 46–47, 52, 127–28
Minimal conflict level, 45–46, 52, 127–28
Moderate conflict level, 47–48, 52–59, 128, 129
Moderately severe conflict level, 48–49, 60–62, 129–31
Mothers, economic and social stress on, 16–17

Neutral drop-offs, 147
Nine-year olds, coping with conflict by, 33–34

"Opportunistic" class of children, 39
Outburst, inciting emotional, 80–81
Overcontrolling personality, 114

Parent(s). *See also* Parental alienation
  child's contact with both, 18
  child's relationship with same-sexed, 16
  communication guidelines for, 137–38
  economic and social stress on mothers, 16–17
  high-conflict, 23
  intensity of conflict between, 19–20
  new relationships of, 150
  rejection of, 65
  residential, child's postdivorce adjustment and psychological functioning of, 17–18
  role as children's protectors, 35
  as role models, 35–36
  subjects of fights between, 23–26
  supporting role of other, 150
  verbal abuse between, 32
Parental alienation, 9, 61, 65–100
  development of, 72–77
    family dynamics, 72–73
    individual dynamics, 73–74
    situational factors, 74–77
  intervention model for, 84–100

children's therapy, 86–90
children who refuse visitation, 95–99
long-distance relationships, 99–100
parenting coordinator, 84–86, 88, 89
strategies for the alienating parent, 94–95
strategies for the targeted parent, 90–94
litigation and, 80–81, 83
parenting coordinator and, 130, 131
recognition of, 66–71
  early, 69–71
tools of, 77–81
  denial and devaluation, 78
  exaggerating unfavorable traits, 79
  inciting emotional outbursts, 80–81
  putting children in the middle, 79–80
  tribal warfare, 79
visitation and, 69–70
Parenting, cooperative, 7–8, 18, 28. *See also* Parenting plan
Parenting Agreement, 136–37
Parenting as ongoing process, 136–37
Parenting checklist, 162–67
Parenting coordinator, 120–26
  children refusing age-appropriate visitation and, 96
  as conflict buffer, 129
  critical goal of, 130
  functions, responsibilities, and roles of, 120–23
  as information conduit, 125
  interview of children by, 151–54
  knowledge of parents' defenses, 123–24
  long-distance relocation by alienating parent and, 99
  parental alienation and, 84–86, 88, 89, 130, 131
  parent-child relationship and, 126–27
  as tiebreaker or arbitrator, 127
  visitation plans and, 127–28

Parenting Coordinator Agreement,
168–70
Parenting meetings, structure of,
133–34
Parenting plan
creating, 119–26
mediation and, 119–20
parenting coordinator and,
120–26
example of, 155–61
impasse intervention techniques,
131–51
behavior modification and practical suggestions, 146–50
cognitive and reframing strategies, 133–38
with "easy-to-victimize ex-
spouse" types, 145
identifying triggers for impasse,
139–45
with "I'm always right" types,
139–41
with "Maybe I will and maybe I
won't" types, 143–45
with "You are always wrong"
types, 141–43
implementing, 125, 127–54
children's input in, 151–54
limiting spread of conflict, 151
for minimal to mild conflict parents, 127–28
for moderate conflict parents,
128, 129
for moderately severe or severe
conflict parents, 129–31
operationalizing terms in, 138
Parenting skills, conflict over, 23
Passive-aggressive behavior, 139
Peer relationships, 15
Performance, academic, 15
Personality(ies)
controlling, 116–17
"easy-to-victimize ex-spouses,"
118–19, 124, 145
exaggeration of defects of, 79, 93
"I'm always right," 111–13, 123,
139–41
impasse and, 106–7
"maybe I will and maybe I won't,"
115–18, 123–24, 143–45

overcontrolling, 114
self-protective, 73–74
"you are always wrong," 114–15,
123, 141–43
Physical abuse of children, 61
Physical violence, 19, 44, 113, 115
Possessions, sharing, 149
Postdivorce sadness, 76
Preference for joint legal custody,
22
Professional help, couples in need of,
44
Psychological difficulties, persistence
into adulthood, 27
Public drop-offs, 147

Reframing strategies for impasse inter-
vention, 133–38
Rejection of parent, 65. *See also* Pa-
rental alienation
Relocation of parent, long-distance,
99
Remarriage, parental alienation and,
75–76
Residence plan, design of, 51
Resilient children, 14

Sadness, postdivorce, 76
Scheduling. *See* Visitation schedule
Second Chances (Wallerstein and
Blakeslee), 39
Self
denial of, 87–88
disorder of, 106
separate, 90
Self-protective personality style,
73–74
Separation, ambivalent, 106
Severe conflict level, 49–50, 62–64,
129–31
Severity of Vulnerability Scale, 108,
109, 123
Sexual abuse, 68
Side-taking by children, 32, 33–34
Six-year olds, coping with conflict by,
31–33
Social skills, 38–39
Special events, 148
Spouse abuse, 61–62
Stalking, 115

Stress
  on children, issues causing greatest, 26
  children's adjustment and parents' levels of, 17–18
  cumulative nature of, 17
  economic and social, on mothers, 16–17
Sudden abandonment, 105–6
Suicide, 117
Supervised visitation, 60, 61–63, 69
Support group for targeted parents, 93

Talk, disparaging, 24
Teenagers. *See* Adolescents
Telephone access for children, 149
Temperament of child, postdivorce adjustment and, 13–14
Therapeutic visitation, 62, 63
Therapeutic visitation centers, 97
Therapist(s)
  parental alienation and, 80–81
  parenting coordinator and, 86
  tribal warfare and, 104, 105
Therapy for parental alienation, 84–100
  children's therapy, 86–90
  children who refuse visitation, 95–99
  long-distance relationships, 99–100
  parenting coordinator, 84–86, 88, 89
  strategies for the alienating parent, 94–95
  strategies for the targeted parent, 90–94
Three-year olds, coping with conflict by, 30
Tiebreaker, parenting coordinator as, 127
Time sharing, 24, 134–35
Transitions, 23–24, 59
Tribal warfare, 79, 104, 114, 141
Twelve-year olds, coping with conflict by, 33–34
Two-year olds, coping with conflict by, 30

"Unhappy, angry, anxious, insecure" class of children, 38–39

Values, shared, 135
Verbal abuse between parents, 32
Violence
  marital, 61–62
  physical, 19, 44, 113, 115
Visitation, 51–64
  children's refusal of, 67–68, 95–99
  conflict levels and, 52–64
    age and, 53–57
    minimum and mild, 52
    moderate, 52–59
    moderately severe, 60–62
    severe, 62–64
  conflict over details of, 24
  delivery of children, 146
  developmental needs of children and, 52, 53–57
  drop-off points for, 147
  makeup time for, 149–50
  parental alienation and, 69–70
  parenting coordinator and, 85–86, 127–28
  sharing possessions and, 149
  structure in, 59
  supervised, 60, 61–63, 69
  termination of, 63–64
  therapeutic, 62, 63
Visitation plan(s)
  adjustment of, 127–28
  design of, 51
  effective, 20–22
Visitation schedule
  age of children and, 85
  changes to, 148
  discussing with children, 80
  irregular, 149
Vulnerability, 107

Wallerstein, Judith, 11, 12, 16
Warfare, tribal, 79, 104, 114, 141
Woundedness, 107, 108

"You're always wrong" defensive style, 114–15, 123, 141–43